*Since
our beginning,
we have been
dissolving
into
nothingness,
instead of
evolving
into
somethingness.
It is
time
to
rise-up!*

The Re-knowing

The Cracking of the Mustard Seed
And the Awakening to the Universal Creator

Gwyndolyn D. Parker

Gwynism Publications

Dedication

This book is dedicated to my family who are the light of my life. My sons Anthony and Nicholas, my daughter Margaret, my granddaughters Juanita and Jordan and my great granddaughter Jayla are the wind beneath my wings and my consent source of inspiration. It is also dedicated to the awakening you.

Acknowledgements

I want to acknowledge my family for their love support and encouragement. My granddaughter Juanita Joy for helping me to proofread, thank you I am grateful. I want to thank all my teachers in the spirit realm. They have continued to assist from beyond, one very special teacher in particular will forever be close to me whenever I write about the Holy Spirit. Without her knowledge and wisdom any research I began would have fallen short, thank you my dear teacher. I would also like to thank the little church that became a beacon of light in the wilderness in my journey for truth. I would also like to thank Metaphysical Universal Ministries for the vibrant learning environment and teaching program for all seekers on the path. I would also like to thank each and every teacher known and unknown that crossed my path and left crumbs for me to follow. They led me down the rabbit's hole to truth.

Table of Contents

The Re-Knowing

Every once in a while
some ancient knowledge
seeps into the atmosphere
of consciousness,
creating multitudes of thoughts
for those
blessed and ordained to hear
why they,
in a predestined arrangement
with the Universe,
are asked
to make a particular knowing re-known,
guiding us to re-think the truths we own
as we listen and hear the sweet knowledge
the Blessed Ones implant in us
sending the new lessons we need
from inside their minds;
for us to impart in the consciousness of humankind
the truths hidden from us since days long gone
of the true love and heritage belonging to an unsuspecting people
in which the "Universe" has always called its own.

The Earth is not flat!
The Earth is not Round!
The Earth is multidimensional, and so are
The Children of "The Most High!"

The Hopi have put us in the fifth realm of existence!

Chapter One

Introduction

My Reflection into the Deep Past...It had been nine months and twenty-one days since I made my entrance into the womb of my Mom. I didn't want to come into beginning here, but the womb grew comfortable and I liked it here. I had made peace with this part of the journey and did not want to leave it. But I was being told daily that it was pass time to go. I was getting too big for the space and for the health of my Mother. I knew that she was walking each day, I bounced around with her and enjoyed the movement, and I had no idea of the toll it was taking on her physically.

Then, the Elders send me a message that I was not going to be allowed to stay in the womb any longer and that I must prepare for my entrance into the world and begin to be the person I was being born to be.

I didn't want to enter this life or to be on this physical plane; I didn't want to breathe air and receive the instructions that came with each breath I took; I didn't want to know all that was in store for me. But I can't say I didn't love my Mom, she sang to me and comforted me; she talked to me as if she could hear my every thought. I didn't want to hurt her, so I had no choice but to go through the birth canal and breathe in the life instructions and start to fulfill the mission placed on me.

It wasn't going to be easy they had not given me a healthy body to live in or an easy task to perform.

I had no idea how scared I was going to be or how hard it was to breath in this atmosphere. My lungs seemed to fail me. I had a terrible sensation of falling, drowning and not being able to breathe all at the same time. The only thing I could do was cry when I could and search for my Mom. Where was she, I had never been apart from her, where was she now, I needed to see her, to feel close to her. My arms were flying in the air, my feet kicked, my face became hot and still no Mom. There was nothing else I could do. Who were these people? They didn't sound like her and they didn't make me feel the way she did. I wanted her, I needed her. It was going to be hard enough to be here, but without her, it would be impossible, I told myself.

I am being moved, where are they taking me, where am I going and where is my Mom, all of these thoughts made me terrified and I began to really worry until suddenly I heard her voice, she said, "there's my baby girl", she sounded weak, but she was my Mom and they had taken me to her. Maybe they weren't so bad after all. They laid me in her arms and I could smell her; and I could feel her; and the world was a little less scary and I could breathe a little better.

We shared something she and I; we shared something that made us closer than normal one might say but being near to her made me feel whole, complete and not alone.

I was born different and only she understood that it was temporary in nature and would not diminish the person I would become but enhance it in ways I was yet to understand, but my Mom knew and began the process of preparing me for the outside world. Yes, we had our afflictions but it was the price we had to pay to be here to do what was assigned to us to do. She was the only person on earth that knew about the journey we were on and she was my only link to home.

My anchor was not in the room and I wailed like a wounded animal, even though, I knew she would return, she always did, I wailed never-the-less the detachment felt so real and the fear grew so strong. I was thoroughly convinced that everything outside of her was evil and harmful and unbeatable that I would become overwhelmed with fear and grief. What if she did not return, what if I was left alone in this cruel world. What kind of world made your body hurt and made breathing hard?

As a child, she always returned and my breathing got a little better and she never complained about the pain in her body.

She read to me from books and papers written by whom she considered great humanitarians. People she considered had much to teach as I had much to learn. So Ralph Waldo Emerson, Norman Vincent Peale, Dale Carnegie, Walt Whitman and the Holy Bible among others would shape my value system and give me the foundation I would need to walk in the world someday.

When you grow-up knowing that you are different, but having absolutely no idea why or what makes you different, you are apt to spend your entire life turning to figure out what it is that makes you different and if it is something to be proud of or is it a source of great shame?

It really doesn't matter, in the end, you just want to know, why your clock ticks differently, why your drum beats differently and why your mind thinks differently than the people you come in contact with?

Once, I became grown and had a family of my own, my Mom was getting weaker and as her physical body was failing her more and more, she began to talk about spaceships and landing sites and began to write strange things that I did not understand. So, I paid little attention and hoped anything I did not understand would go away.

I wish I had paid attention at that time, she had answers to the very basic questions I had asked so many times and as her body was failing rapidly and twilight was setting in she was trying to set the record straight and give me what she knew as her remembrance was returning to her. After her final ascent, all I had was her black speckled notebooks to give me answers.

The books became a roadmap for the journey I would later take in search of answers and awareness. I had no idea, she knew about Pyramids, Stonehenge or the Great Wall but she did. I had no idea she knew astrology but she did. I had no idea, she knew about the blood but she did. What I didn't know was were the "Blood" came from, she did not get to write that in her books, but silently, I promised her I would find the source, and with that promise the hunt was on. She had taught me never to make promises I could not keep, so I couldn't start to do that now.

Time was on my side, she had always said, "daring to be different is a really good thing, embrace it, it is your legacy". Being different would definitely help me to think outside the box, because if it was inside the box, I would have to look for it. It would already be known.

So I embraced being different, while at the same time striving to be normal, much fear and anguish resulted from the juxtaposition of these opposing desires.

The journey to awareness was strong and even at the end of this book; I will not be able to tell you how my journey will end.

The journey did not start out with a known destination. I had no idea what I was searching for, I had no idea I was searching, I just knew that there was something I needed, I did not have.

When I was very small I would search for a church to belong too. I wasn't aware of religion at the age of six or seven but I was aware of the church buildings and I wanted to go in and see if it was my church. My mother never said no to me. She just got my clothes ready for Sunday morning, making sure my shoes were shined, and my dress was starched and ironed just so. A nickel was ready for the offering and at the appointed time, so I wouldn't be late, I was off to the next church in my neighborhood. It seems, as I reflect back, that I was always in search of a church to call home, and a place that would give me what I was in need of finding. At six, I did not know what I needed to find, at thirty-six, I still did not know what I needed to find, but I had decided that books might help and had started as a child to amass an impressive library of non-fiction books on any subject I thought I was interested in, mostly religious and historical works. In them, I found many answers, but those answers only led to additional questions, and the search was never concluded and the questions never really answered to my satisfaction.

You would think I would know how to start this story I have chosen to write, but time and time again, I start yet another first page, always trying to get past the beginning and onto the heart of the story. The story I want to tell is about me but it could also be about you, if you are African-American or a black person from any country in the world. This story may also be about you and a history that is not widely known to the average person. So, maybe if you are an average black person then this story may be of interest to you. But then again, if you are a history buff and the historical timeline from the Greek doesn't quite make it for you, then maybe there is something in this book for you. Or, if you love religion, like I do and have some questions on the early church fathers, then just maybe this book is also for you. If you have always wondered about blood types and their origin then just maybe this is the book for you.

I am going to try to answer the questions that from the age of six I must have wanted to know. I am going to do my best to satisfy my quest for the answers and maybe along the way I will answers yours, or give you some direction or insight so that you can refine your search and continue on your own quest.

My journey is divided into searches for my ancient heritage, my bloodline, the one true church, and the idiosyncrasies that my family, a peculiar people and complete who I am.

As I said my journey started with the search for my church. Somehow I must have thought the moment I entered it I would know it and feel at home immediately. Throughout my childhood and all the many churches I would enter, I never found that at home feeling. The church of my Aunt and Uncle was the closes, but I knew it was not my church, even though I didn't know why. It was a search that would continue for decades.

The search for the one true church led to the search of my ancient heritage. Why didn't the western churches give me what I was searching for and what was it that I was searching for that they could not give me? I am black, black people come from Africa and to Africa I must look if I want to find me. Until I understood who I was I would not know why I had a need to know anything.

Then, there is the origin of the blood and the bloodline that I have not been able to explain. It should have been the easiest one to explain, but that did not turn out to be the case. Now I am beginning to see why it is taking a lifetime to get to the bottom of some very simple questions. Who am I? Where did I come from, and why do I seek a church I cannot even describe?

Trying to explain this to you will not be easy. I have tried with many, many starts to this book from many different angles. Each seemed right at the time. Each was yet another start, from another point in time, and sometimes from a different memory or point of view. But all of it is true just now written in chronological order or if it is, is not finished, it stops with nowhere to go, because most of the time, I left something out, my focus was off, it was too narrow.

I think I can now incorporate the many starts into the first part of the book, and then really reveal what I have discovered in my journey of self.

Being inquisitive naturally, and having what seemed to some to believe that I had an unhealthy interest in things, as I might have thought to be self- absorbed, but I was not, just deep in thought. There was a real quest for knowledge and answers that was really buried deep inside me, even though I didn't know it then. I was compelled to search for it, as if driven by forces that might have had move interest in knowing than I did.

All I know is that even if years went by and I allowed myself to live a normal life and just be in the world doing everyday normal things. I would eventually be drawn back to the quest for the answers of the thoughts that would pop into my head. I would be off to the library to do research and come home with an arm load of books that had to be back in two weeks.

I have often described my search as trying to connect the dots, following the bread crumbs; but more recently I have termed them clues from the "Thoughtland". The Thoughtland belongs exclusively to God. It originates with God and can only come from the "God-land", of the Most High heavenly realm. These clues are helper agents, for humanity's search for self, and are only there to aid in your search for a better you. If it were harmful to your higher self, it would come from a different source and be designed to aid in your demise not your advancement.

My explanation for writing this continues…

If I were to tell you I was born to write this, you would question it. You would be right to do so. In fact you should question everything. Everything that you have been taught, everything that you have been told, should be questioned. You should leave no stone unturned, because much of what you have been told is a lie. Even the truth is tittering on the brink of untruth. From the very beginning, you have been force fed a version of reality that suited someone other than yourself. You have been instructed on how to live within that reality based solely on what was presented as truth and as fact to you. You accepted it without question and as absolute truth, so your world view was formed and the dye of your norm was cast. Now, I am not saying that I welcomed this task of being the truth teller, but I was nevertheless tasked to present this knowing to you. It took a lifetime for me to get to this point. For it is not easy to have your eyes opened to a truth that is hard for you to comprehend, let alone accept. My view of everything had to be pried open before I could adopt the habit of seeing what did not want to be seen. But once you get there, there is no turning back. There is no white without black and there is no gray without a mixture of white and black. The world you suddenly live in is full of muddy waters, dark caves and caverns, musty books, and translations from weird languages unknown to most of the world's population; and you go down a rabbit's hole you can never crawl out of.

Trying to establish a work of non-fiction just because you know it to be true is both tedious and wearing on my patience. I simply must tell you what I know deep within in my soul to be true and let you find the truth in it for yourself. So I am declaring this a work of non-fiction that has yet to be proven by you.

It was through this vantage point offered by ancient knowing, some spiritually fed; some from books that mysteriously showed up; and some from mystics just crossing my path that I decided to just tell you a story and let you brand me a charlatan or a heretic, if that is what you are compelled to do. For I know from experience you cannot un-ring a bell that has been rung. You can't un-see a truth that has been shown. So let those that have eyes to see, see, and ears to hear, hear.

We begin with...

I have a collection of bibles
in my search for something
to help me understand
but not finding it
I continued to collect
Bibles,
commentaries,
bible dictionaries,
and interpretive books.
The search was endless
it literally caused
a slow dig into
the
center
of
existence!

Chapter Two

Beginning the Journey

Let us begin with the bible...

There are concrete reasons why I was chosen for this journey. I had the task of learning about the bible and life in general began when I first arrived on planet Earth, even if I didn't know it.

I am an introvert by nature and an inquisitive soul by birth. I could and would wonder endlessly about the human condition, or about the way a stranger looked or acted. I would take it as far as the imagination would let me. The outside world would eventually get in the way, and I would be forced to return to the reality of the moment, but I never quite saw things the way others saw them or accepted them. I never really thought life was ever the way it was presented to me. I was convinced it only seemed that way to others, but why, I didn't know. It was almost as if I could see the cracks in the veil of this universe we were trapped in. There was something missing, I could feel it, I could almost see it, but not quite. However just that little bit of knowing would forever lead me to search for what I did not know but could feel deep down in my bones.

As a child it was easy to think this way, but as I grew up the world of right and wrong, good and bad, white and black did not allow me time to entertain the fantasy worlds of missing things and unanswered truths. I had passages to memorize, computations to master, and tests to take. Then there were degrees to get, jobs to work, and a living to make.

In reality, the cracks were still there, I was just no longer able to concentrate on seeing them until the day when my religion kicked in big time, and all of the old unanswered questions, thoughts and opinions resurfaced like cold water on my face.

The Original Bible

The very first thing I am sure of is that the original bible is older than dirt- meaning it is utterly out of this world, and has only been accessed telepathically by only a few beings from the establishment of time. A written connection between humans and their God was never necessary as long as they were spiritual light beings. It was only the deep descent from the light that made written knowings necessary, less they lose their way back altogether to the source from which they came...

However, the pure written language of the Heavenly realm is now only in the Akaskic Library, which houses every thought and every utterance from the Universal mind and humankind. Still only a few have access and ever fewer can truly disseminate some of what is there. The bible alludes to the ascent of Enoch into the Akaskic library and other heavenly realms, in a statement that simply states Enoch was taken-up in a whirlwind.

The book of Enoch which was either removed from the bible or never incorporated into it, tells a much fuller story of the taken up of Enoch and what he learned and what he saw. The book *the Keys of Enoch*, is so advanced that only scholars of science, engineering, astronomy, and astrology are in a position to grasp some of the details of this advanced science. Future advances are still being worked on from the "Keys", but we are not there yet. The teacher for this will come when the student of humanity is truly ready and not before.

Having said that, where we are now, in terms of our education on the earthly realm is this, everything we know about our world, ourselves, our ancestors, and our heritage should come from the ancient writings in all their many forms. The forms that are comprised of but not limited to the many languages presented in the form of cave pictorials and art; the many varieties of early writing forms including cuneiform which still has not been fully made public. The hieroglyphs as found carved in stone and printed on papyrus leaves and every other surface that could be used to record history from the oral tradition. But, the question we need to ask here is has everything come from the ancients or has everything been altered to advance a very different reality?

When it was decided that a history and an accounting of life needed to be recorded for the next generation or for the next....it had to rely on the different forms of writing that had developed over time, and thus formal languages from the base language were developed. We are not told what language was the base for the languages we speak today and without knowing the base, how can any assertion of truth be held as absolutely true?

Out of all of these mediums came the interpretation of everything we have to draw from, except for those hidden books and documents deems not for our knowledge and not for our preview. There are many secret documents and many records that would shed light on truths we have not been told, and many things that would reveal lies we have been told. They are hidden in vaults, archives and libraries not open to the general public. These documents, artifacts, tablets, scrolls, books, music, and literature of all types lie hidden from our view. They are spread out around the world, as if to make sure they are never all found and pieced together. The fragmented history has been left as non-contiguous pieces to be categorized as anything any historian deemed them to be at the time. The few famous and honest historians were seen as outliers to the mainstream thinking of the day, and therefore great for advanced studies, but not applicable to general studies, since it went against the narrative of a tightly controlled world view.

How was this Possible?

The questions aren't only why and how was this possible? But for what end was it necessary to bury factual history?

Why? Because the documents of old tell a very different story than the one we have been told, and shed a very different light on the past, which would change the present and the future of humankind and dismantle their tightly held accounting of everything.

It is quite interesting that the most widely circulated book is actually based not on fact but on the "new" truth presented by the new conquers of the immediate area, at the time of the critique of the "new" history and the story's formulation. There were areas of the world they had not discovered, had not visited, had not introduced their "new" truth too, these areas continued to use the language of their ancestors, and practice the faith of their ancestors as they had done for thousands of years before. The ancient history and its recordings of its history did not change because there was a new power structure in Africa. Life went on for thousands years more, and in some areas continues to this very day.

The people of Africa had spread to all areas of the world. Their influence had encompassed India and well past India, as well as all through Africa from east to west, north and south. They then took to the seas and no island or landmass was off limits, so monuments to their presence and in their likeness continues to exist as testimony to the first human's blackness. Yet, we were led to believe that outside of Africa, anyone's blackness was due to the sun, and had nothing to do with genetics. This knowledge has been accepted by the ruling and governing class as some sort of gospel, even though there is no logical way it could be true. If you take a black person to live in Antarctica that person would never turn white. It is only through the mixing of the people of different hues that create a change in color in subsequent generations, but not of the individual itself.

We are not supposed to connect these dots but we will, and we will be enlightened by the knowledge that all that glitters is not gold, and what you see is not always all there is to see.

Therefore, we were deceived in the knowledge of the, who, what, and how the islands and, so many of the continents were populated with blackness. Blackness was everywhere long before slavery. Although many islands have never been bound or related to slavery, yet their populations have their base rooted in blackness.

We have been carefully taught not to question, we were told to respect the scholars, without ever asking where their information came from; or asking how they formed their assumptions, we were told not to ask just accept it as is. But if they had documents to back up every assertion, and if such documents exist, why can't we read them and see for ourselves, what the Ancients had to say? Why can't we all be as smart about our heritage as the scholars?

Is it Tucked Away?

Why does the Vatican house documents and books no one is allowed to see? Why did certain religious scholars demand to see any newly discovered religious artifacts, before the public, and why did it sometimes take years or forever to release it to the public?

It may have been questions such as these today that presented much the same backdrop eons ago, when scribes were commissioned to work for the very rich and the much empowered class, that the "new" bible was written. There were many prophets, scribes, and historians writing about life as they knew it in the days of the new bible genesis. But in truth, the day of the writing tablet was a very long time before the time of the new bible.

For there was the time before time, when the language of the original bible was based on a language of love, you could sing it like a love song, for it was a love story between God and her children. The *Songs of Solomon* have even been whitewashed to make us believe that the use of the word black did not mean black and for centuries we were lulled into believing what we innately knew to be false, that those words were not written about a white woman, for there has never been a time when a white woman has ever been called black and comely. I will discuss a little more on the *Songs of Solomon*, later in the book.

It was a kind of loving discourse on maintaining an intimate relationship with the Light, to ensure a shield against any negative forces, as well as a way to stay focused, balanced, and aligned in right mindedness.

The revengefulness, which is very much a part of the Old Testament, was not a part of the original bible for it was not an emotion that the Creator wanted to evoke into the Children of God.

Hate is not an Original Emotion!

Hatred was also a foreign emotion and not one present in the Children of God. Love was the emotion and this emotion was extended to every living creature on the face of the earth.

The original biblical writings that today's bible draws its best from, are inspirational passages gleaned by the most spiritual ancients of old who were only able to keep the smallest fragments of the love and sweetness of the original works in the bible.

Today's bible represents a fictional story, of a fictional people, that wants you to believe was there at the beginning. This bible wants you to believe they knew God. This bible wants you to believe that the Son of God was born 2,000 years ago and whose linage can be traced to people and their linage here on earth.

Of course this is simply not true. They will never tell you where the Son of God came from because if they did, then that knowledge would throw the entire biblical account into question. The fairytales of the bible to justify murder, thief, and usurpation would be exposed as ill-gotten gain without any rights of ownership.

The stolen inheritance as recorded in the bible would be exposed, and as in any legal court proceeding, when wrong is exposed, reparations are levied as judgment, and restitution is demanded. Can you image if restitution was demanded from 2,000 years of recorded servitude of the earth's population. Can you also believe that the book used by the prosecution to indict is the bible itself, which was created to make their false claim in the first place?

This "new" bible should come with a warning label that reads: the names, places and people have been changed to obfuscate the real people and their story. It should further state that entire books and nations of people have been removed to inject a new people to take their place, their life, and their history.

It should also warn you that the names and places have changed and do not in any way, shape or form reflect the biblical people of the original bible by name, country of origin or skin color. The most famous couple in the bible that is so misrepresented is Abraim and Sari; they were the true Adam and Eve of the bible. The promise that God made to them came true as evidenced by all the brown and black people on the earth today.

Another very important fact to note: God does not make mistakes, but man however always does. God did not change anyone's name; there was no reason to do so. Man however did, and said it was the work of God. How absurd! I find it hard to believe anything when it starts with the premise that God said to change the origin of the Children of God into a different people of a different time. This was and is an absolute red flag for me.

Simply put, instead of preserving history, they buried it, for a newer more modern version more to their liking.

Where are the Keys?

There are key words in the bible that pertain to the way God decided to choose, set apart and identify the children of God. They were called from the beginning the *elect*, the *chosen* and the *sealed*. It doesn't matter that these terms came to mean something very different in later times. The original intent is all I am interested in conveying to you. There is a great need to clarify, and bring forth, that which was hidden from you.

It was not a religious sect that decided who was *elect*, who was *chosen* and who was *sealed*. It was God and it was a part of the beginnings which no history has accurately recorded.

The bits and pieces of that bygone era is recorded in Genesis, but without the additional writings of ancient manuscripts, the other missing books of the bible and the mythological texts, stories and lore, we will not have a complete and accurate picture of the true nature of God, or of the world, its people, or the true creation story.

Probably, one of the biggest mistakes of the biblical scholars was the taking of science and anything deemed akin to it out of the bible and out of the norm, for it was and is a part of the norm in all of history. To deny its existence in the bible as heresy was to decide not to include certain books of the earlier bible, and exclude hold groups of people because of their contributions to science, engineering, astrology, astronomy, and agriculture, namely the Ethiopians of old. Without this group of people in the mix, the scribes' historical account does not square with how things could logically have happened.

There are major chunk of space between what happened before the beginning, what happened in the beginning, and what happened at the time of recorded history of people actually living on the earth. This very statement came to me over many years of wrestling with the gaps in history, I could not reconcile.

To determine and pinpoint a place to begin, I think it will be helpful to lay some foundational understanding of things, for these things are absolutely necessary, in the building of a new knowledge base.

In the next chapter, we will explore some hidden or obfuscated knowledge. It is knowledge that has always been hidden from the vast majority of people in the industrialized world, and in particular western civilization. We will explore these revelations through a series of questions that will most certainly need to be pondered, analyzed and discussed in intimate settings, large forums and hallowed halls, but never again in secret.

Exposure to things
not discussed in our childhood
or adult life as a matter of course
is the very definition of
Hidden knowledge;
Hidden knowledge provides
different definitions of things
not widely shared
with the general public,
but some hidden things
can serve to re-awaken
our understanding
of the universal self,
in a way that will anchor truth in our soul,
and allow our own knowing to come forth.
It will rewire the brain for critical thinking
and crack open the Mustard Seed!

Chapter Three

Recognition of Hidden Knowledge

Definition: Bible

The dictionaries have very unique things to say about the bible which contributes to its wide appeal and amazing sales on a global scale.

The Bible is reported to be by Guinness World Records to be the best-selling book of all times.

The Bible is considered to be the inspired word of God, it includes 66 books written by about 40 authors and is written in three languages on three different continents over approximately 1,600 years.

The word Bible most likely comes from the Egyptian port Byblos where papyrus was used to create manuscripts and scrolls which were later taken to Greece. The other names for the Bible included Holy Writ, Scriptures all meaning scared writings.

The Bible covers topics such as love, fear, humility but it also gives in sometimes great detail war, corruption, incest, cruelty, homosexuality, adultery, lust and every weakness that has befallen human nature. It is a book that leaves nothing out and nothing to chance except it doesn't tell you not even once how such a complicated book written by so many, over such a wide range of time, on so many subjects is to be correctly interpreted.

The Good News Book has been kept alive and a valuable source for a reason, no book no matter how shored up and preserved will be read unless there is something of value in it.

The Bible is very valuable but the average person does not know how to read it, except I suspect some of the elderly, who had long since stopped reading the words as words and just starting feeling the spirit of the unspoken words.

How can one accurately interpret the Bible?

First, by understanding how the Bible was written and rewritten over the 1,600 years.

There are seven levels of understanding woven into the entire collections of books within and without the Bible. The seven levels are:

Literal

This is the interpretive level and is design so that you can be taught to read the Bible in the most basic way without explaining that there may be metaphors or allegories presented, not just a historical story. The reader reads it has actual fact just as presented.

Exoteric

A level insures that the teacher has a form of writing that is suitable to be imparted to the masses, that which can be given for general consumption written for those outside of the inner circle.

Esoteric

This Level has deeper meanings and is intended for a much small group of those with inner restricted knowledge, exceeds what is seen and taught on the literal and exoteric levels is designed lay people.

Gematria

This is an important level for there is a systematic coding of words, phrases and positions hidden within the verses of the Bible that hold scared meaning to those who have knowledge of such things. While they are hidden in plain sight without the knowledge and the secret inner knowledge they go unnoticed and unchallenged by the ordinary reader. From cryptography, cabala, and numerology certain words and phrases take on whole different meanings and understandings to different groups of scholars and historians.

Alchemy

This level of knowledge pertains to ancient chemistry of a very spiritual nature as in the transformation of matter and the turning of base metals into gold, a form of transmutation.

Metaphysical

This level blends science, astrology, time and space to find the cause and source of everything. It assumes that science cannot be left out of spiritual things because it is a part of the foundation of all there is.

Spiritual

Divine spirituality, is a state of consciousness that transcends all other levels, and enters into the realm of Light at the highest levels of human understanding and capability on the earth plane. If one can read the Bible from this place, eyes see, and ears hear what is not shown and what has not been heard by others who are not where you are at that moment. While this experience may not and for most does not last, it is amazing while you are in it. It is akin to what happened to Enoch but on a smaller scale as one can imagine. But when you are privileged to see beyond the veil and beyond your comprehension even for a brief while, you will never be content to be spoon fed the mundane explanation of anything ever again; just as Enoch was forever changed you will be as well.

The Bible is an extraordinary book; it is widely circulated and read by billions but most are still at the base level of interpretation while the transformative power of alchemy is at their fingertips and they do not know it.

Divine Spirituality is the station that gives sight to the blind, hearing to the deaf and empathy to the hurting and allows you to actually feel what it is like to walk a mile in someone else's moccasins.

Access to the Divine Spirituality in the Bible is hidden from us and it must be uncovered.

Hidden Knowledge

After reading many books of the Gnostics, it became abundantly clear that the bible did not deliver the complete teachings of The Christ. In fact it seems that bible scholars went out of their way to minimize his teachings into a few sound bites. Just as they indeed did minimize his life, so as not to have to explain the real who, what, how, and why of his being; his very teachings had to be kept hidden as well.

In the beginning of the history cycle, the sacred writings were revered and thought not to be for the general populace, and were from the historical beginning of our modern record keeping kept secret and hidden.

At the time, I did not look for what the deeper meanings of this oversight might have been, but now hindsight has kicked in big time.

Learning to Seek

A saying attributed to The Christ by the Gnostics "Be as wise as serpents and as innocent as doves," may have many meanings, but one interpretative meaning might be that in order to discern what was left available one must have an open mind and a discerning mind. The kind of mind needed to see beyond what is currently available to review. But, the seeker's mind also has to be an intentional truthful mind, not one wanting to know for nefarious reasons, or idle musings and purposes. One must have a noble desire to unlock the secrets of the Universe, for only those who have ears to hear and eyes to see beyond will be privy. Many did not know this and are still stumbling around in the dark.

The saying also reveals something about the symbol of the serpent and its place in the story of the Christ. Serpent knowledge, which throws the entire serpent in the Garden of Eden story into question, can it be as simple as "ignorance is bliss", the reason that hidden knowledge became taboo in the Garden because it attributed knowledge as the reason for the fall of mankind? Is the symbol of the serpent, which was the symbol of ancient knowledge as described in many ancient manuscripts so detrimental, that it had to be villainized through lies to kept ordinary people from seeking to know it? By association, did the Garden of Eden and the Children of the Light also get become scapegoats?

The repression of ancient knowledge became the order of the day, instead of the intended passing of the knowledge from teacher to teacher and then from teacher to the lay people (us). We were always supposed to know about the whole life and teachings of The "Christ Energy".

We were supposed to know so our knowledge wouldn't be diminished as the Christ Energy of the Living God became a tiny speck in the vast universe, leaving us without the complete knowledge of how we could individually commune with the Most High God and bring about our ascension internally.

We were reduced to needing intercessors and mediators to act on our behalf and we were supposed to believe they were honest brokers wanting only our salvation. While in all actuality they were holding us hostage for ransom payments and obligatory services to prove our worthiness to them, and not to the Most High.

Getting to Wisdom

What we are left with now is a need to understand this, which is: knowledge leads to understanding and understanding leads to wisdom. This phrase has a literal and a metaphysical meaning. It is just one of the many things that will change the way you look, decipher, and react to the universe once you have ears to hear and eyes to see.

We cannot be blind to learning. It is the key to rising above everything that holds us back from reaching our full potential. Understanding what is presented to us, is also a key to unleashing the abilities already within us to rise higher. But it is the obtaining of Wisdom that assures us that ascension is ours, for wisdom comes with the indwelling of the Holy Spirit. Once you have received the indwelling you will not and can never be of the world again, for you will emphatically know that you are only in it for a while.

You learn that words and phrases in the bible have meanings far beyond the literal understandings – we lay people have been told.

To gain a greater understanding, I continue to research the Gnostic writings for insight. I am forever grateful that I did. For from that moment on, not one passage read in the bible by me, or passages read by biblical scholars, bible teachers, or clergy was ever received by my ears the way it had been previously heard.

Each phrase, word grouping or significant word in the bible has a knowing attached to it that is important to our understanding of the pathway home. When these pathways are obfuscated and kept hidden from view, we are not able to rise above the murky darkness of our current existence and connect to a greater source of light. Each word or phrase when properly activated is associated with a musical note and color and is honored and recognized by the Universe. They have the ability to change the DNA sequencing of the activated individual allowing them to once again correspond with their higher soul family and the process of ascension begins.

Our local leaders and principalities of Earth have no desire for anyone to escape their grasp of complete domination and control, therefore constantly wage war on individual enlightenment. We are not to know that this is not supposed to be our forever home. We are not to know that when you die an earthly death, you are not dead.

Into the Weeds

Now I present some new thoughts, definitions and explanations I have gleaned from my research, and from the intuitive knowing, I received from the indwelling of the Holy Spirit, for your preview and hopefully enlightenment. Why? Because some of our old definitions will no longer satisfy our understanding of what is real.

They have told you that Jesus "The Christ" lived thirty-three years. They told you in vague generalities, about a boy at age twelve and a man at age thirty. They gave a small sampling of his teachings, but not enough for you to fully grasp what he really meant by their literal interpretations. The Gnostic writings offer deeper insight, and bring new meaning to some foundational key words and phrases we have heard in religious centers from the beginning of our religious experience.

One of the things they did not tell you was that anything relating to the supernatural aspects of "The Christ" were ordered taken out of the bible by the rulers of the new world, which had to be an attempt to disinherit you from your from your rightful place in the Kingdom of God.

The deeper we go the more you will thirst for additional knowledge. Insight is so contagious. You can acquire your rightful inheritance, if you are still breathing, it is not too late.

More on Hidden Things

So...why were there hidden things?
Under the Greek Philosophers there was a genuine desire to articulate a philosophy of their own. The abundance of information they had to rely on came from the vast libraries of Africa, which were like none, any other civilization, had ever seen.

I know you have heard of the great library at Alexandria on the Mediterranean Sea, but the real truth is that the library in Alexandria was just a repository, commissioned by the wealthy to retrieve, confiscate, and deliver the intellectual manuscripts from libraries and universities in other known areas of Africa, areas that remained untold and not talked about for thousands of years.

The manuscripts included works from the most ancient and knowledgeable people to ever grace Earth, and are the basis for everything we know today. This knowledge also included an introduction to future sciences that have yet to be fully deciphered and understood. A few enlightened ones have gleaned some insight from information that lay dormant for lack of understanding have gone on to do great things such as Tesla.
This planet we call Earth is still young in its knowledge of science and human evolution.

Plato, Socrates and Aristotle have presented the ancient philosophies as their own, and as such, we have been content to believe that the foundation of our intellectual Knowledge, of all there is, had a fundamental Greek background, which by every account simply is not true.

Greek history and its interpretation of history might as well be called a modern representation of history but not a factual account of history for accuracy standards.

Historians will readily admit that there are gaps in the interpretations of the manuscripts and other documents they have tried to decipher, which has happened either because:
- Some of the manuscript is missing
- They were unable to translate some of the text
- It was foreign to their level of intellect
- It was at odds with their social morays at that time in history

Historians in those days were not known to be without bias. Alas, there were many manuscripts that were not translated at all and many that never saw the light of day. Many of these hidden knowledge bases have never been debated or seen by the noted scholars of today, which has left a large vacuum in the knowledge of what we try to comprehend today.
I need to establish that we cannot take on the whole at once, but must take it on, phrase by phrase, sound bite by ancient sound bite. If we are to be able to advance our understanding of what was not provided.

But first, I must state that the Holy Bible is a modern day name of the book that supposes to house the word or Logos of God.

The book is actually the words of man, who never knew God. For if they had they never world have changed the language of love to the language of hate and revenge.

If they knew God, they never would have deleted words of God and injected people, places and things as the words of God, in order to invent a story not germane to the nature and image of God.

But since they took ancient manuscripts and text as their foundation, we can still glean valuable insight if we just parse it out, one phrase at a time and "be wise as serpents."
The key to understanding hidden knowledge is not to dwell on the big picture, but to meditate on what jumps out at you, or something that nags at you every time you see it.

It is simply a knowing that tells you there is more to this than is meeting your eyes, more than what you have been previously told or exposed too.

When this happens, it is because you have received inspiration from the "Thoughtland", or the Universal Mind of God.

When you start your research you will be amazed at the gifts you will receive from the Universe. You are not alone in your quest for the hidden knowledge of the universe.

All that is hidden will come to light!
An interesting fact to emphasize my assertion is the *Original Sinai Bible* the oldest know bible has over 14,800 differences between it and the King James Version of the bible. After learning this fact, my first question was why? My second question was why have I never heard about this book before, I was in Mount Sinai and did not hear about it; I studied the bible, collected bibles, and still did not hear about it, why?

Why should we care, the book is certainly big enough already, right? Wrong! The book leaves out some very important information while as the same time asking you to believe without question.

You are asked to take it word for word without question as the word of God. But if it was the word of God, why would any word of God ever need to be deleted?

You are told not to question what you read, when it is obvious that someone else already has.

So it doesn't stand to reason, that seeing the two books side by side, is a better way to judge a book by its content?

Tips for Effective Biblical Discernment

You now can see that the bible is full of a god that is not our God. It is full of violence revenge, and retribution for sins that are committed over and over again. It is full of things that have proven to be ineffective strategies at best.

The original word of God has long been lost in the world. Today, you can only find a literal morsel here and there of the original word or thought.

You find a few crumbs of truth and a little tidbit to wet your whistle which drives inquiring minds to want more, but to get more you have to do a few things.

- Go within for the answers you seek
- Read the Word for meditation purposes
- Ask questions and meditate on them
- Seek learning from spiritual leaders that are led by the Holy Spirit
- Learn to recognize answers as they flow from the higher spiritual realm
- Train your mind to seek goodness in every answer
- Prepare yourself to be still and have eyes to see and ears to hear

*Cracking
open
the
Mustard
Seed
to
reveal
the
truth!*

Chapter Four

Cracking Coded Terminology

Uncovering some of the hidden knowledge!

Cracking the code of the mustard seed requires the researcher to parse the phraseology, determine the real definition, untangle the allegories, demystify the symbols, and ask the questions needed to get to the answers the seeker seeks.

We know that the church has always known and been privy to a greater wealth of knowledge about our past, knowledge that was never transferred to the exterior body of the church. I am also certain that the 4th century AD 325 first Ecumenical Council held was to establish the foundation by which all in Christendom would indeed worship under. And so the outcome of the convention was the creed.

Nicene Creed of 325:

"We believe in one God, the Father Almighty, Maker of all things visible and invisible.

And in One Lord Jesus Christ, the Son of God, begotten of the Father, the only-begotten; that is, of the essence of the Father, God of God, Light of Light, very God of very God, begotten, not made, being of one substance with the Father, by whom all things were made both in heaven and on earth; who for us men, and for our salvation, came down and was incarnate and was made man; he suffered, and the third day he rose again, ascended into heaven; from where he shall come to judge the quick and the dead.

...And in the Holy Spirit.

But those who say: 'There was a time when he was not,' and 'He was not before he was made;' and 'He was made out of nothing,' or 'He is of another substance' or 'essence,' or 'The Son of God is created,' or 'changeable,' or 'alterable'--they are condemned by the holy catholic and apostolic Church."

This paragraph was placed in the creed to dissuade anyone from disagreeing with the creed as Arius did. Arius was a Berber which was the original people of today's Libya. He was also a highly regarded priest in Alexandria, Egypt of the church of the Baucalis. His teachings were in direct opposition to the "God in three persons, holy trinity" and taught that the Christ was created by God and is separate and subordinate to the Father. He presented this argument at the First Council of Nicea, and the rest is history. His belief system Arianism is considered a nontrinitarian belief system and was not welcomed in Christendom.

The Creed which came out of the Council of Constantinople in 381 AD:

"We believe in one God, the Father Almighty, Maker of heaven and earth, and of all things visible and invisible.
And in one Lord Jesus Christ, the only-begotten Son of God, begotten of the Father before all worlds, Light of Light, very (or true) God of very (or true) God, begotten, not made, being of one substance with the Father; by whom all things were made; who for us men, and for our salvation, came down from heaven, and was incarnate by the Holy Ghost of the Virgin Mary, and was made man; he was crucified for us under Pontius Pilate, and suffered, and was buried, and the third day he rose again, according to the Scriptures, and ascended into heaven, and sits on the right hand of the Father; from where he shall come again, with glory, to judge the quick (living) and the dead; whose kingdom shall have no end.
And in the Holy Ghost, the Lord and Giver of life, who proceeds from the Father, who with the Father and the Son together is worshiped and glorified, who spake by the prophets.
In one holy catholic and apostolic Church; we acknowledge one baptism for the remission of sins; we look for the resurrection of the dead, and the life of the world to come. Amen

I recited this as a child. It was in the front of our bibles and recited every Sunday morning. I thought it was honorable and good and worthy of the God I served. I was a child then, but now I have put away childish things in order to truly serve the Most High God.
In each creed if you look closely you will find a veiled reference that is disconnected from the body of the text but for some reason they were still compelled to place it somewhere, as if for further reference or because it would render everything completely false not to include it somehow. The phrase is "And in the Holy Ghost" in the Constantinople Creed, and in the Nicene Creed it ends with a standalone sentence, "And in the Holy Spirit."

I was blind but now I see, I was deaf but now I hear. It was in 325 AD that we were carefully taught not to question any doctrine coming from the Church and its clergy. We were so carefully taught and we were good little sheep.

But it is now time to wake up and become the true seekers we were awakened to be.

So with this in mind, let us now discuss some hidden knowledge in the phraseology references of the bible and other Gnostic books; let us also do some redefining of some popular definitions, and let us ask some questions, that people are bound to have asked and have pondered during their lifetime. But, most of all bread not crumbs should be available to the hungry, just as water is to the thirsty.

Throughout the rest of this book I will try to offer you a bounty of wheat to make your own bread.

Phraseology: In the beginning...

Genesis 1:1
Maybe it would have been more accurate to say in the beginning of
something new.
The statement encompasses many knowings and also many questions.
> The question is in the beginning of what...?
It tells you of the existence of something higher but nothing about the how,
the what, or the when. Therefore I contend that the beginning was more of
a forward leaning statement than an historical one.
> 'In the beginning' says more about when the new realm of reality
was created than a starting point of all that is and ever was, for surely we
can all agree that we will never know all.
This is the salient fact that many miss when reading the bible. Life has no
finite beginning and no finite ending, and Earth is not all there is. But by
misreading the first sentence many religious scholars have cheated us out
of the most important foundational knowledge of our lifetime here on
earth.
> So the very first statement you read in the bible actually takes you
on a wild goose chase through the entire book, to pinpoint our existence
into a fixed placed in a fixed time with a fixed purpose, which has led us
away, not toward our higher purpose.

Phraseology: Let those who have eyes and ears!

> In the Gnostic book *The Gospel of St Thomas* Jesus said: "I shall give
you what no eye has seen and what no ear has heard and what no hand
has touched and what has never occurred in the human mind."
> The narrative of the verse stated there was nothing new under the
sun but that there were secret things hidden in plain sight.
> I can believe that. I also believe that while there is nothing new
under the Sun, there is plenty above the sun that has never been brought
down to earth. Therefore, however much there is on the earth plane there
is so much more above. There is so many different ways we are constantly
being persuaded that here is such a wonderful place, that we forget this is
only a stop in our journey home. It is not the end stop, just a stop.
> The thought of this just being a part of your journey home is all
that you need to stay a seeker and have the will to become clear eyed and
real hearing enabled.

Definition: Thoughtland

It is through an absolute desire to connect to the Most High Source that one can draw near enough to hear, feel, and know beyond one's present comprehension the thoughts of the Most High.

Once you have removed the barriers and obstacles in your path, your thoughts are connected to Source and your desires are made known. This is when you have eyes to see and ears to hear the answers the "Thoughtland" manifest to you.

Embracing knowledge from as many sources as possible will lead to the wisdom needed to enter into the Thoughtland. No one gets there by accident for it takes intention.

Be Still – be peaceful become centered, settle yourself to be able to have eyes to see and ears to hear words and/or inspirations that are meant to help you discover the answers you seek to find your true path, calling or purpose, that will help you to draw ever closer to the Most High Source.

If it is a closer walk you seek; if it is a better understanding; if it is answers to the burning questions about who you are, and what is the meaning of your existence, then make your way to the "Thoughtland" for the answers lie there and are waiting to be revealed to the true seekers.

Phraseology: As Above so below

The phrase, "As above so below" was a real puzzle for me from the moment I heard it. As above what, where and so below what where? That was the literal me asking, but when you get to the spiritual question, you discover the truth. The hidden knowledge conveyed in this phrase is so very important to our understanding that I wanted it to be one of the first phrases we looked at.

Also though this phrase is not mentioned in the bible that we use it is widely used and understood in the writings of the Gnostics and is considered basic knowledge in the Spiritual community.

It exists to give us a basic understanding of our connection with source. We are not disconnected and left alone in the universe. Once we know that from the very beginning we were not alone but connected by our thoughts, actions and deeds, it behooves us to act accordingly, and by working to understand more about the Creator and our connection; to trying to understand how to become more like the Source.

Nothing that happens on the planet earth by those connected to Source can happen unless it is first conceived of, by thoughts in the heavenly realms. Earth is the manifest station of the thoughts of heaven. All of our thoughts go up to heaven, and come back to us manifested through the power we have to create that which we desire. This is the reason why it is so often said, be careful what you wish for.

But there are also other meanings to this phrase such as the Creator of above creates the begotten of above, just as the creator of below creates the children of below.

There is much symbolism to explore in this statement.
There are those who did not come from this earth, nor will be returned to this earth. If you came from the stars, you will return to the stars. You will indeed return from whence you came from. This is a true and binding statement.

Remember the saying "ashes to ashes", which means for some the spiritual fire will burns off your physical body and to the stars you will return.

Whereas "dust to dust" simply means to the earth you will return, physical body and all.

If you look out into the universe at night you will see that darkness is all around, but you will also see the light twinkling and illuminating the night. The darkness gives birth to the light as it gives reflection to the light.

So it is on Earth, we are in the darkness but we (the Children of the Light) are here to be a reflection of the Light.
The terminology "As above, so below" is part of the Immutable Law, the Law of Correspondence, which is a Universal Law. It is also one of the reasons that no earthly ruler can indeed win in the end. The Light will always prevail.

There is more on the Immutable and Mutable Laws later in the book.

Definition: Soul

We are a soul living within a body. The body itself is a temporary vehicle made just for us to use while here on this planet. But we will still be a soul long after the body has expired.

The growth of the soul is the ultimate aim in existence to grow beyond the physical and return to the spiritual. Our goal is to evolve out of darkness and transition into the Light.
The soul is tied and sourced from the Eternal Divine Source.

If you are seeking the path
Rejoice because when the student is ready the teacher appears.

If you have a sense of why you are here and it has anything to do with the betterment of humanity rejoice because you have earned knowledge of the purpose of your soul.

Rejoice because The Most High has already smiled on you.

Rejoice because you are already following your divine path.

Rejoice and walk with joyous steps in the path that pleases the Most High, because the path you are on betters humanity and works to advance it forward and you are already in serve to the Most High.

"I know who I am, and I know whose I am!" is working within to become clear to you.

Definition: Time

Time is a construct developed for the sole purpose of marking the experience of everything on the earth plane. Time is a measurement of material creation. The planet earth is a material creation.

However, there always was and are realms of existence where there is no such measurement of time. Realms where the construct of time has never existed and never will, are also located in some of the realms we call either the heavens, or the many mansions or the many universes.

Hence the words eternal and mortal, earthly existence is a time of being mortal, and as in Shakespeare, it has its exits and entrances, but in the Heavenly realms death is not known and existence is simply advanced and ever evolving.

I only know of three time periods, but the Hopi know of five. Although, I can't see the other two, I do not doubt for a second their existence.

The time before time is about the House of the Most High and the family of Angels

The Second time period tells of the time of life on earth when both the family of God and the children of man occupied the Earth

The Third time period is what we are in now. It began when the Prince of Darkness became the ruler of the lower heavens including Earth.

What has confused me is the fact that history and historians cannot, or have not reconciled these time periods; cannot pinpoint accurately the key dates of occurrences, and of key moments in earth's history.

There are instances were events are intertwined and meshed together, further maddening the already murky waters. So, by giving you these three time frames, you can freely determine for yourself, when something doesn't fit with the narrative you are reading, in which time period you think it belongs.

It seems the scholars struggled to disseminate some information they gleaned because of competing theories and noted thoughts of other renowned scholars, which increased the uncertainty of what we thought we knew.

As historians struggled with current history, ancient manuscripts and mythological lore to see the truth in our humble beginnings, they were forced to realize it was no easy feat and nowhere near humble.

Yes time, the presence and absence of are very important to the telling of the existence of Humans on the planet Earth.

Definition: Multi-dimensional Human Being

We are created with mind, body, and spirit making us three dimensional beings sharing everything with our host. It is at birth, when we breathe in the breath of the Most High that we receive our own unique identity and encoding in the soul.
Some scholars believe that the soul dies after death, while others believe the soul never dies.

The Christ's teaching teaches us that both are true, the soul of the children of the Light continues on in the cycle of evolution.
However, the soul that was created here on earth has no such inheritance to everlasting life and if it is to continue must seek the Light and renown all claims to the darkness. If this is even possible, of this I am still not sure, to be very honest.

It is the eternal Soul of that advances in the other realms of existence and out of this material construct, we call earth.

Definition: Mankind

The use of the term mankind is a product of the male paternal system put in place in the scholarly teachings, but is regarded as a collective for having a sin nature and a product of the Sons of Darkness.

Why on earth would we ever refer to the collective beings on this planet as mankind, when every single person was birthed from the womb of a woman?

This alone is enough to make everyone question the birth of humanity and the use of the term "mankind"; it was never referred to as "womankind" neither is acceptable terminologies.

We are human beings with both male and female qualities and attributes, which cannot correctly then be lumped into a category that does not allow the whole self to be present and accounted for as a human being. Therefore, the correct terminology at that time would have been humankind.

Phraseology: Mustard Seed

How will the Children of God have knowledge of their inheritance and of their importance as a stranger in a strange land? They will not unless they go within and with the faith of the mustard seed that was placed there, let it grow until it becomes the Mighty Oak it is supposed to become.

The knowledge placed inside of us symbolized as the grain of a mustard seed. A small kernel of faith which we can use to ignite the light of all there is under the sun. It is up to us to own it and grow in the light from within where it has been placed. The outside world does not want us to find the light within, but the power lies in us to find the hidden treasures of the light.

Once placed, it will withstand the test of time, and is readily accessible by the Creator to be groomed, nurtured and loved throughout eternity. If it was not here, you will not know it, but without it the Creator will not know you as its own and an inheritor of eternity.

The mustard seed is also symbolic of the "spark of light" described in the bible. This spark was given to the children of light that they would never be without a piece of their creator. I think it also serves as an identifier where in Matthew 10:30, it states ..."*but the very hairs on your head are all numbered.*"

This was also a hallelujah moment for me!

Phraseology: Be in but not of this world

For those who are called the Children of the Light, who are identified not by name and form but by the soul and the indwelling of the Christ-Spirit; this knowledge resides in the soul and the soul has been known by God since before the foundation of the world. The Children of the Light are only a traveler passing through like those who have traveled the Merkavah in the Holy Gospels, who will ascend and descend through the aeons of time doing the work of God for his pleasure as written in Ephesians

Important to note that being in but not of involves spiritual detachment of the interior journey and gives the soul access to the world of Godly Light or the many worlds of God or the House of many Mansions. As spoken of in the bible. You may say this Earth is just a pit stop in a great and wonderful sojourn.

Owning eternal life really does mean seeing this existence as a learning experience, not an end, nor a beginning, just a stopover of the continuum of life and its many forms.

Phraseology: Stolen Birthright

There is a big different between selling something and stealing something. The Bible uses both examples to show how the birthright of the chosen was acquired.

However, the birthright of the "chosen," can neither be given away or stolen away.

A birthright given by God is forever for it pertains to having direct access to the heavenly realms.

A stolen birthright on earth however, is another story, for it can only pertain to earthy things; earthly dealing, and was expressly used in the time of the second earth age.

Things on earth can be sold, stolen, or exchanged as you can do with any material goods, but an inheritance from God is not transferrable and stays in the family from generation to generation until the end of time.

The second earth age attempted to usurp all of the things of the first earth age an incorporate them into their earthly history and culture, to validate their existence and establish their right to the inheritance and ensure the admiration and obedience of the people.

Therefore, it was for this reason that the Children of the Most High God had their birthright stolen when those who were not of the Light came to the Garden and stole it from them.   There is a preponderance of evidence in science and in the bible to lead one to this conclusion, yet we continue to rely on current day morays to explain ancient knowledge and wisdom.

It is important here to remember that the garden was the entire earth plane. It is also important to point out all of the landing strips and navigational instruments used to plot the course of the stars, was available in ancient times as depicted in hieroglyphs on temple walls in Egypt. We have never been alone in the universe. From the very beginning there were watchers from distant stars and even today someone is always watching, hovering, wondering what we will do next. But, we continue to disappoint. How long will we be allowed to continue to spiral out of control, before a reckoning is required?

Definition: The ALL

The ALL which pertains to the definition of God in the bible is a very revealing statement when you look at it from different vantage points.

ALL, nothing missing, nothing broken, means all inclusive, having everything within, needing nothing external.
Thus, the Alpha and the Omega as stated in the Bible, complete from beginning to end.

The one true thing that we lay people can take away from this re-knowing is that there is not and never was a need for The ALL to use humans on the earth plane to create anything and certainly not a God. Therefore, if there was an Immaculate Conception it happened before the foundation of the Earth and before time and space was created by The ALL.

The story of the Immaculate Conception was a story told in the Second Earth age to retell an ancient story and reinterpret the truth into something very different.

We have all loved the iconic manger story but it simply did not happen. But, it brought the iconic mother into a narrative of the new earth age with a kind of worship that didn't include the actual energy of spirit, or rightful place of importance. Instead as a religious symbol it was a way to have a collective worship, which could be easily controlled, steered and corralled. It allowed space for any remnants of the past to remain intact as they could now be explained away or be put into a new context, as well as validating any claims that were made.

The ALL is inclusive of having the ability to create infinitely! Therefore, if the ALL actually was tied to earth, would the earth be in the mess it is in today?

Definition: ARCHE

ARCHE means the beginning; the source of all things, in Science Fiction they have used the term architect of the universe to describe the source.

In Genesis 1:1 the first words "In the beginning…" brings this term to light as the source that made all things.

Logos "word", the hidden order of all things as is the Harmonic with its numerical ratios in mathematics. It is well known among Hebrew just how important words are in mathematical relationships in the universe, everything is related and balanced through numerical correspondence.

Doesn't the word Harmonica just perk up your interest? In this one meaning you are thus aligned with the music of the universe and its corresponding mathematical equations, which mean that everything scientific aspect cannot be ignored or dismissed for it is valuable to our growth and evolutionary progress.

Music and math are a part of who we are and essential to establishing a way to re-knowing how to connect to Source.

Harmonica is the harmony of numerical ratios in mathematics. Your brain juices should be flowing just reading this. It should because one of its meanings is its alignment with the music of the universe and the corresponding mathematical equations.   This therefore means that the scientific aspect of all nature cannot be ignored or dismissed because it's basic relevance to our growth and evolution. To successfully deny the relationship between us and science is to lessen our ability to draw closer to Source and our re-knowing. Simply put it deems our light and weakens our connection to Source.

The further removed from the pure language of the time before time; the more confusing the explanation of The Most High becomes, which since the beginning of time has gone from a benevolent loving, kind, gentle inspirational "ALL" to a three dimensional being housing force, might and exacting revenge.

Definition: Beginning of Life

Ezekiel 37:1-5

Life begins when the first breath of God is drawn, not from the mother, for it is a one to one connection that remembers the "soul" to God and it is at this time that the "soul" is imparted into the being. The bible says for life without the Breath of God is just flesh.

From the womb of the mother to the womb of God, until the cord is cut detaching the child from the mother and the first independent breath is taken there is no life affirming human being for the child must be part physical and part spiritual. The first breath outside the mother's cord, enact the soul of the new born and instantly creates a golden cord attachment with The Most High. Until this occurs there is not a Godly connection that includes the possibility of eternity.

In Ezekiel, it also refers to rebirth, which in spiritual circles is called reincarnation, which pertains to eternal life.
This is another re-knowing of the relationship of "As above, so below". We have a divine relationship and everything is connected in ways we have yet to recognize and comprehend, so when you hear the saying, "we are all one", for some of us this is true. We must now learn to recognize our true brothers and sisters.

Definition: The Two's

There is a running narrative in the bible about two's. There seemed to be a need to create duality as an acceptable attribute in the biblical story telling. Thus instead, of telling the history of the heavenly age, which included a connection with the first earth age, and then telling the story of the second earth age, it has glossed over the different ages, and fused the very different histories into one confusing narrative. Hence we have duality in many and varying forms.

The most famous example of two's is Cain and Abel which is probably an amalgamation of the two Angels, the two Adams and the two brothers Jacob and Esau.

Noah's Ark where everything entered in twos, this of course is a fantasy story but it is a way to explain how the new earth was repopulated after the first earth age passed away.

The two Angels, the Bright and Morning Star and the Daystar; Michael and Gabriel

Two earth ages could this explain dimensions and alternative universes?

Two Hebrew Priesthoods Levi and Aaron

The Old Testament and the New Testament

Two Gardens of Eden

Some of these will be discussed more under their own heading. The very fact that the duality exist without clarification in the bible, a book that we have been taught to take at face value, and without question boggles the mind and adds injury to insult.

...and thus the mystery continues to add fuel to my burning desire to dig deeper.

Phraseology: The story of Jacob's ladder

Genesis 28:10-22

The story of Jacob's ladder is very important because contrary to popular beliefs, it was not a dream, or an allegory, but a description of what took place between the Heaven we know nothing of and the Earth's beginnings as it was being built by the Children of God.

Jacob's ladder was foundational to the building and creation of everything that was built, placed and formed on earth at that time. It is still evidenced by the many monuments, temples, statues that are still present on the Earth today.

It was not a dream that Jacob had but a real life occurrence of the travel of those we call Angels from the heavenly realms to the earthly realm as they traveled back and forth building, establishing, forming, installing things on the Earthly Garden of Eden.

Yes, here you have it Earth was the original Garden of Eden and the entrance to the Garden of Eden was in a particular place on Earth which I will get to a little later.

Phraseology: The Fall!

The "fall" and separation of man and the angels is well documented in many Gnostic texts, while at the same time, is also well hidden by obfuscating almost all of the truth, and creating a fictional account so easy to deny.

Modern text does not explain how these two groups managed to co-exist in the heavenly realm or on the earth plan. Although clearly they were connected and a major split occurred.

But, I do know that it was the angels that were the creators of all that things we have today that we cannot explain. The reason that we can't say it is just maybe it would open Pandora's Box, and out would come all the many things that were hidden from view and explained in a very different way.

At some point, there was a certain intermingling of angels and humans who was expressly forbidden by The Most High, which is mentioned in Genesis 1:11, again in Deuteronomy 7:3-4 and in Hosea 7:3-4. It was to no avail, I guess it is true that opposites attract or what we are expressly told not to do, are the things we want most to do. In any case, there was intermingling with disastrous result. It is knowledge, that only The Most High, and the heavenly hierarchy knew, but apparently was completely unknown by the angels or the humans on earth.

The Gnostic tell of the angels taking human women as their wives and of the creation of off-springs who had considerable more power than had been envisioned for the first earthly human population.

The power to create without an understanding of anatomy, relevant consequences and a plan to reserve any adverse effects was apparently not a conversation that had been given to the humankind population. It was one that the angels understood and disobeyed, hence the "fall" of the angels.

This "fall" meant that certain angels that had freely traveled back and forth between heaven and earth were no longer able to do so, and their powers were confined to the earthly realm forever.

I cannot imagine that anyone knows the real story about what happened after the flood, but the one we have been told is not the real story either.

Phraseology: The Apple

One thing is clear; the story of the apple and Eve is false. Women have been carrying the burden of the Adam and Eve story from the beginning of the biblical account of the story. It had made its way into the core of everything we know and hold dear. Women have been objectified, marginalized, scapegoated for the sins of the angels, who were told to leave the daughters of man alone.

This turned into the fault of women. Why you ask? It seems that we did not get rid of the remnants of the angels after the flood after all. For if we had a very different story would have been written, which is another reason to question any references to the flood story. Everything that is taken literally in a symbolic book has a tendency to have disastrous consequences.

It is interesting that in hieroglyphs on temple walls in Egypt, you will find the legend of a god changing into a crocodile. I'm thinking that this would have been a great way to survive the flood and reemerge on the land again.

But the story doesn't really answer the question and hold up to the scrutiny of broad daylight, so something is still missing.

Here is a clue, the line in the bible, "not one dot or tittle or law will change until heaven and earth shall pass away", and so the first earth age had to pass away, along with the first Adam and the first "Rapture" had to take place. But since any rapture would have to have been a supernatural event, it all had to be rewritten to fit the new narrative. We were left deaf, dumb and blind to the inner working of the Holy Spirit which was our link to the vast workings of the Cosmos.

Definition: The Flood

The first earth age ended with the flood. The flood itself is a metaphor for a cleansing and what happened after the cleansing is a new beginning or a new earth age, where the clock is reset or time and space is reset or changed.

It was in this period that the bible could rightfully have called the exodus for it was the official end of the magical Garden of Eden. The beautiful first earth age had ended and only the knowledge unearthed later would tell of its grandeur.

In the second earth age, people were no longer immortal nor did they enjoy a long lifespan and they no longer had the assistance of the Angels to help them bring whatever they wanted into existence.

Remember the saying in the Garden about Adam having to work and Eve having to bear children? This did not exist in the first earth age for everything was created in a begotten sort of way, this all passed away with the end of the first earth age.

For the first time humans were cut-off from the heavens and alone on the earth, at least they thought they were alone. All of the decisions made were made by them and they were responsible for their own actions.

In the flood, the cleansing, the great circumcision took place when some human beings where disconnected from The Most High. Circumcision is not of the flesh, it is of the spirit for they had gone the way of the "fallen".

Spiritual separation is the absence of the light from above hence the Children of the Darkness ruled the earth in the second earth age.

Definition: The Two Gardens of Eden

Earth came into being billions of years ago according to scientific sources, but it became the Garden of The Most High when the decision was made to place "life" on it.

Making a planet habitable for life with all of the abundance necessary to sustain life is described in the bible, and the earth certainly has everything needed to have life abundantly.

When the first earth age passed away so did the first Garden of Eden as they were one in the same.

In the second earth age according to the bible, the garden was a small place on earth not the earth itself. It is very telling how the scholars of the second earth age disavowed science, astrology and astronomy. Therefore, they were not able to think in terms of the true vastness of the universe, for without science, it was well beyond their comprehension.

What we have in the bible is the amalgamation of the two earth age stories of the Garden of Eden without recognizing that there cannot be an accurate telling if first we don't recognize the two earth ages and the important connection of As above, so below as a constant thread through our connection to the Universe.

Now that we have the ability to fly drones in the sky, with high definition cameras that can hover and capture the true landscape below, we are able to see more landing strips than were previously known to anyone. Some ancient landing strips are under water some high on mountain tops which could only be seen, all at once, from above. These findings topple everything previously believed about travel between our world and other universes. It is no longer science fiction, but unknown history.

Things have emerged to foster new knowings of the intelligence of the early ages of the humans living on the earth plane, in stark contrast to the stone age we are supposed to have descended from, these new knowing fully debunk the six thousand year theory.

While it is true that there was a Stone Age, it was only in the second earth age, never in the first. Stonehenge is a great testament to this fact for it is far older than the second earth age. Stonehenge is actually made of some type of metal, just covered with a stone surface to represent the Stone Age.

The second Garden metaphorically describes four types of people as descending from the four rivers pouring out of the Garden of Eden. However, since those of the original garden were made in the image of the Most High and were not a part of the same group that populated the land in the second earth age, the combining of the two gardens presents an incorrect picture.

Definition: The Two Angels

Michael and Gabriel are the two most important angels mentioned in the bible.

It is said that Archangel Michael is the one who defeated the angel who waged war in the kingdom of The Most High. The angel he is said to have defeated has been called Lucifer and Satan. There has been great controversy over the hierarchy of the Luciferian contingent, but Archangel

Michael has remained constant throughout recorded history as the defender of The Most High. It is also said that Michael is The Christ of the Age and in this age is referred to as Jesus the Christ. What is important to note is that all of this happened in the spiritual realm. The realm without form, for all was spirit until the time of the great deception. Therefore any mention of the First Christ was of a spiritual nature and of a spiritual time.

Archangel Gabriel had the title of Messenger of The Most High. The bible states that Gabriel was the messenger that delivered the message to Mary that she would conceive the immaculate conception of The Christ.

However, if Michael is perceived by scholars to be the Christ already, then Archangel Gabriel could not have delivered that message from The Most High. Here is where a new thought seeded from the "Thoughtland" came into being. If there was no need for The Christ because he already existed, then what was Gabriel really doing with the daughters of man? The Angels were explicitly told not to enter into the daughters of man, so why did Gabriel go to Mary and why did he need to have his own immaculate conception? Who would it have been that whispered into the ear of Eve in the garden?

There has never been a reason before or since for The Most High to invade a human's personal space, and second, there has never been a reason to send a messenger. The Most High needed no intercessors to communicate. Therefore this is where the Gabriel messenger story falls apart for me, but it has allowed the Archangel Gabriel to fly under the radar and remain relevant and revered throughout time.

There are so many people that believe in angels who have allowed deceptive messages to be delivered, and believed in as coming from The Most High.

The stories of twos continue to play out in all of recorded history of life on earth and life in the heavens as it pertains to human life.

Could it be that Gabriel was really the fallen angel, the messenger of The Most High that did not follow the message?

Was the war in the heavens waged between the followers of Michael against the followers of Gabriel, and is Gabriel the leader of the third of the angel kingdom kicked out of heaven and descended to the earth realm?

Did Gabriel become the Prince of Darkness in control of the earthly realm? Did Gabriel set himself up as LORD?

Is Gabriel's message to Mary in the second earth age his attempt to duplicate the heavenly realm with a Christ of his own? Is this where the saying the begotten of man came from? There is a great deal to ponder here. I have questions, so many questions.

Definition: Cain and Abel

The story of Cain and Abel is probably older than the dirt of the earth for it is the same story of the two's told and retold down through the eons of time.

The bible speaks of The Bright and Morning Star; the bible also talks about the sons of the morning; the bible also talks about the Day Star. In my youth I spent time trying to make sense of the nagging questions this presented to me. I totally abandoned the search for the truth as I really just got more confused with each try to untangle the web that was woven. But now almost a lifetime later it is much clearer to me. From the temple hieroglyphs the story of Osiris and Seth as told thousands of years before the bible was written, to all of the mythology stories about the rift between the brothers that has been played out over and over again. I now think it is the telling of one story, the story that happened in the beginning... you know the gap of how things were before the six days were completed.

There is still a war raging on earth between those of the Light and those of the Dark. One of the most important things we may need to understand is the two Adam's. They are the end result of all of the other two's, but are the ones we most identify with now as we are all supposed to be descended from and linked to them by the bloodline of the Christ, but does our linage come from the Bright and Morning Star or the Day Star?

The two are not the same but everywhere are referred to as the sons of God, just as Cain and Abel were sons of Adam; just as Osiris and Seth were sons of the Gods; just as Jacob and Esau were brothers, all were polar opposites and so it is today. Right here, there are still polar opposites factions, raging in the world today for power and control of the worlds resources. It is done with no regard for human life or the quality of human life against those that value all life.

We are here on earth and the bible says that the first will be last and the last shall be first. The Bright and Morning Star was first the Day Star will be last. Matthew 19:30 and 20:16 was a reference attributed to the Christ to his disciples. This statement although we have no real understanding of exactly when it was said or to whom it was really said, is of great importance on its own merit. For it still relates back to the two earth ages and the first and second inhabitants. What if this statement means that the originals of the first earth age will return and assume their rightful place again?

There is great meaning in this knowing and we must know the difference between those who say they are believers in The Most High and those who continue to try to usurp the position of those who truly are the servants of the Most High.

Phraseology: Receivers of the Biblical Inheritance

Before the foundation of the world those created in the heavenly realms as the begotten of what we call God received the inheritance. This happened before time and before space, when all was one.

The inheritance was supposed to go to those who worked diligently for The Most High in the creation of the Earth plane and were faithful to the word and wishes of The Most High. Although we will never know how long there was no division between the heavens and the earth. But, it seems that envy came into the hearts of some of the angels as they looked upon the children of the Light with envy and rebelled against the word and wishes of The Most High and stole the inheritance of the earth, but they could not steal the children's inheritance of eternal life.

In Ephesians 1:11-14

In him we were also chosen, having been predestined according to the plan of him who works out everything in conformity with the purpose of his will, [12] in order that we, who were the first to put our hope in Christ, might be for the praise of his glory. [13] And you also were included in Christ when you heard the message of truth, the gospel of your salvation. When you believed, you were marked in him with a seal, the promised Holy Spirit, [14] who is a deposit guaranteeing our inheritance until the redemption of those who are God's possession – to the praise of his glory.

If you don't pay any attention to anything but the message and not who is supposed to have said it, or to whom it was supposed to have been said, it is still a pretty wonderful find in the bible.

My heart sang praises to God when I first read this many years ago. Even though at the time, I wasn't absolutely sure what I had stumbled upon that made me so happy, I knew it was a great knowing, it leaped into my soul and my inner knowing and it was the first time I knew that the original bible was older than the dirt of the earth.

Look at the words chosen, predestined, plan, you believed, marked, seal, guaranteeing inheritance, God's possession. Clearly it was a designation that was earned for some reason, but the foundation of the world and destined to last for throughout time.

Phraseology: Circumcised

The circumcision refers to what happens to the heart when a karmic cleansing takes place to achieve a free flow of Kundalini Energy, according to ancient Sanskrit text. It does not mean anything of a physical nature for anything physical only pertains to the Earth realm and does not have any effect on the Spiritual realm. A person who obtains a spiritual circumcision is freed from anything that blocks their ability to access a connection to The Most High at will. We use words such as meditation, prayer and being still, it all needs your will to activate the connection.

All things of The Most High do not have a physical hindrance for it is only measured by the spiritual attributes of the soul.

We are told let go of the flesh and negate things of the flesh and because of that the whole conversation always takes on a sexual undertone, which leads people to think that sex is the culprit. It actually is a reference to the lower five senses that keeps us somehow stuck in an "I, me, and myself" kind of mode.

But thinking that flesh is tied to sex and is therefore the root of all evil, and therefore somehow inadvertently linked exclusively to women as depicted in the story of Adam and Eve, Hercules and Jezebel, and other symbolic representations of women and sex as the downfall of man. All of this has nothing to do with the symbolism of physical flesh. The symbolism ritual has been used to define the Chosen, to define the Eight Day, which correctly relates to the second earth age, for the first earth age was seven days long.

The circumcision meaning of the first earth age was strictly about the clearing of the soul from the karmic hold of the earth and fully aligning with the Eternal Source so as not to be tied to the desires of the physical form over the spiritual form.

Definition: the Snake

The snake symbol in the bible is the symbol used to do accomplish several different things at the same time.

The scholars, instead of saying, that an Angel of The Most High came into the garden to beguile the prototype of the human race, turned it into a snake.

By using the example of the snake which was also the symbol of the Tree of Knowledge of all Hermetic Teachings, they made the snake a villain and taboo twice. There was a third important thing that happened, and it was the blaming of the breech in the garden on Eve instead of laying it at the feet of the Angel of The Most High who had strict orders to stay with their own kind.

Four important things happened in the beginning, during and end of the end of the first earth age:

1. The Snake which was a symbol of learning and knowledge became the symbol of evil which helped to plunge the children into darkness for lack of information. Knowledge and learning was left to just a few and deems wrongful for everyone else. Remember knowledge leads to understanding and understanding leads to wisdom, which leads to awakening.
2. By blaming the snake instead of the Angel of The Most High it allowed the Angel to continue to operate freely and to mislead the populace from that time to this very day.
3. It created a female villain that has tainted the feminine energy in both physical and spiritual form since the being of the second earth age. This would not have happened in the first earth age because The Most High was still connected to the earth realm and the flow between the heavens and the earth had not been closed.
4. A fourth thing that happened, as a result of the first three, was a switch in the second earth age from a maternal to a paternal society. So much damage continued to plague the feminine that she eventually lost her power and the right to the linage of her line. But if truth be known it was severed in the garden when the bloodline was tainted with bad blood.

Definition: The Chosen

Most think that the chosen were chosen in earth time and the earthy realm, but it is just not true. The bible is very clear on when the chosen were selected.

The verse of Jesus above lets you know how small their numbers are, but they are chosen for a purpose and no one can self- select this title. It must come from above. "Many are called, but few are chosen" is a true statement, but it belongs to the earthly realm of chosen and is in no way related to those chosen by God. Followers of Christ may choose and have developed methods for how they have choose to become the chosen by man, but only God chose the original ones mentioned in the bible.

The chosen by God follow a certain path some call the continuum of the Light via the journey of the soul. The bible recorded this journey through the generation and covenants in the Holy Scriptures of the first earth age in Genesis Chapter five.

Why is this important, it is because the continuum is another way of saying that the chosen have a continuous connection with the Most High, one that cannot be broken no matter how many lifetimes one evolves through. It also means it is unconditional which means it is not based on merit or good behavior, but on God's Grace and Mercy.

Ephesians 1:3

The Children of the Light have been blessed with all spiritual blessings bestowed upon them by the Most High.
The meaning of blessing in this context means to speak well of;
Since God is the one acting in this verse, we can say that God has spoken good things about us, or pronounced good things for our benefit. The good things that God has decreed for us are probably beyond our ability to number, but we can outline a few by looking at the verses which follow the statement

Ephesians 1:4-13

The first blessing listed is the election as saints. Ephesians 1:4 says that He has "chosen us in him before the foundation of the world, that we should be holy and without blame before him in love." God has chosen to make us holy and blameless, and all because of His love, His good pleasure and His grace (vv. 5-6). What a blessing, that "even when we were dead in sins", Ephesians 2:5, God chose to extend His grace to us and offer us salvation! This is even more amazing when we realize that the decision was made before sin had even entered into the world.

Definition: The Elect

Jesus said, "Blessed are the solitary and elect, for you will find the kingdom for you are from it, and to it you will return.
What has never been explained to a lay person is that the soul has two parts,
The Academy of Future Sciences believes that the children of God have two souls:
- The earthy soul which they call Nefesh
- The heavenly soul which they call Neshamah
There is one soul which belong to God and one which belongs to the earthly realm. All souls come from the Kingdom of God and are destined to return to it. Only the souls that are unified and redeemed, ransomed from the cosmic forces of ignorance and reborn of the Holy

Spirit, who has become solitary and elect received his or her Neshamah or heavenly soul and returns to God's kingdom.

The Nefesh returns again and again to the worlds of admixture and darkness until it is reborn of the Holy Spirit and joined with the Neshamah and is redeemed.

The two souls' idea may be a nice way to explain a complex issue, but it doesn't mean it is true. I have not been able to come to agreement on this in my mind, so I just present it to you for your own further investigation.

There is also the two cord theory the golden cord is said to forever linked to God and what is God's will return to God, while the silver cord upon death is cut. This ties in nicely with the two souls' theory. Render unto Caesar what is Caesar and unto God what is God's and the battle for souls continues, with the most important question remaining unanswered. If there are two souls how can Caesar acquire the golden cord or the heavenly Neshamah, and if you are elected, how are you exempted from Caesar's grasp?

Definition: of the High Priest of Salem (Melchizedek)

In order to fully understand and appreciate the High Priest of Salem, certain other definitions also have to be flushed out.

What is a High Priest?

The honor bestowed on one whose love of righteousness and peace are above reproach and who is willing to be sacrificed for such beliefs, is the best explanation I could come up with. So this is a placeholder for a better explanation. I do not buy worldly definitions but will rely on divinely inspired ones.

What is Salem, where is Salem?

Salem was a name for the Heavenly realm and Melchizedek was the High Priest of the Heavenly Realm having been given that title by the Most High God.

Why was Melchizedek call Priest of the Most High God?

The best explanation is that this destination was given to the one who stood up for and defeated those who sought to overthrow the Most High God. Because of his loyalty and selflessness, he was given the title and the responsibility.

Why, was it the first use of the term "Most High God" mentioned in the bible?

This is a term used to further to the Creator of the many Universes and realms of existence. In the spiritual realm such a distinction was not necessary, but in the earthly realm with so many little demi gods, one finds that there is a great need to distinguish between the lesser and the Most High.

Why was Melchizedek's lineage important?

How was it different than other important figures in the bible?

The fact that Melchizedek was without father or mother, without genealogy, without beginning of days or end of life, and would remain a priest forever is the most important statement about his existence. It is very important for our understanding of everything relating to the time before the beginning and the time after. It tells us that the passages in Ephesians are the foundation for this statement in chapter 1 verse 4 which states:

Even before he made the world, God loved us and chose us in Christ to be holy and without fault in his eyes.

So the children of the Most High God were created before the world was created and were without sin, for God saw no fault in them. Created beings did not need a mother or father for The Most High God had the ability to create with thought, by fiat and by the WORD of God! I know it was a lot for me to comprehend as well, in that it took a lifetime. But nevertheless the statements in the bible about such an important knowing did not come easy to ferret out. Yet, Ephesians was always a particular favorite for the statements about predestination and before the foundation of the world; being holy and without blame; made according to the good pleasure of his will.

Ephesians 1:4-6
According as he hath chosen us in him before the foundation of the world, that we should be holy and without blame before him in love: Having predestinated us unto the adoption of children by Jesus Christ to himself, according to the good pleasure of his will, To the praise of the glory of his grace, wherein he hath made us accepted in the beloved.

What drew me to Melchizedek in the first place?

Why is the relationship between the High Priest and Abraham important in the placement of earth ages?

The relationship of the High Priest and Abraham are significant before it establishes Abraham as being before the foundation of the world as well. It establishes Abraham and Sarah as the blessed to be parents of many nations in the earth realm to come.

What attributes of Melchizedek are noteworthy?
- King of righteousness
- King of Salem
- King of Peace
- Without mother or father
- Without genealogy
- Without beginning of days or end of days
- A Priest forever

No other Priest is mentioned in the bible before Melchizedek, making him the first and the only. He was established before the foundation of the world was even a thought in the mind of the Most High God. No one that came after has the same pedigree, rights and privileges no matter how closely emulated they are.

What is the difference between The High Priest of Salem and Jesus Christ?

The High Priest of Salem was created before physical form was needed and when immortally was certain and before the need for genealogy was necessary before all belong to the Most High God as their only source.

Jesus Christ was born in the earth age to a mother and a father, no matter how divine the written explanation was it still cannot match the authenticity of the High Priest of Salem whose very genealogy was recognized even in the bible itself as having no mother or father in the traditional sense of earthly space and time.

Therefore Jesus Christ was an earthly creation and even though the Christed One exists still in the High Priest of Salem because he is a priest forever. Whatever fiat is decreed will stand the test of time. I am not saying that the world does not have a savior; it is just that, it is time to know the absolute truth and the obfuscation of the truth, for obfuscation can get you into trouble.

What do we know about Abraham?

As stated Abraham was placed at the time of Melchizedek; therefore it places them both pre-beginning times. This will become even more important later.

He is said to have paid tithes to Melchizedek which in hindsight cannot be true because there was no tithing in the spiritual realm. This seems to have been placed there as a way to bring the tithing practice forward and give it legitimacy in the earthly ages. In the spiritual realm all needs were met by thought and not hard manual labor. Manual labor did not come about until the discretion took place in the garden which clearly was in the first earth age.

This places Abraham well before the time of the Levi and Aaron Priesthood, and well before the Exodus mentioned in the bible.

Why isn't Sari Abraham's wife ever mentioned with the building of the nations? It is not as if Abraham could go it alone. Sari and Abraham were the original Adam and Eve in the Garden of Eden and they were the parents of many nations throughout the world, as was in accordance with the will and purpose of the Most High God.

There is a passage about going to a far off country and I think this was Sari and Abraham's entry into the Garden of Eden of Earth.

The conventional wisdom that we are descended from Judah can't be right for none of that existed at the time of the Priesthood of Melchizedek.

At some point, the two different time periods were fused together to create a very different view of how things were, even though they were unrelated facts and unrelated times and events.

When rewriting history and trying to force the pieces that you want to fit that don't it is like trying to force square pegs into round holes, there are cracks all over the place. I am seeing light through those cracks. *Hallelujah!*

Definition: The Rapture

There was a rapture that occurred in the earthly realm and it happened just before the separation of the heavens from the first earth age. It was recorded as partakers of the inheritance of the saints in the light who has delivered us from the power of darkness and translated us into the Kingdom of his dear son.

There are some inaccuracies in the statement, but for now it is enough to know that historians have recorded the translation of saints into the heavenly kingdom.

Those that were translated are described as being:
- A chosen generation
- A royal priesthood
- A holy nation
- A peculiar people
- Who were called out of the darkness

The Serpent Symbol that led the spiritual beings away from the Most High God is described as:
- The prince of the world
- The prince of darkness
- The prince of the air
- The father of lies
- A murder from the beginning
- The corrupter of humankind
- The author of the separation from the Most High God
- The origin of the original sin

You can understand now, why the eventual separation of the heavenly realm and the earthly realm was necessary to maintain the sanity of the kingdom of the Most High God.

When word of the rapture was gleaned by the ancients of old they longed for such an occurrence to happen for them as well, and to this day there is a longing for a rapture to take place and rescue them from the perils of the darkness of their existence here on earth. But without the proper information and the proper guidance, their waiting will indeed be in vain. For it was correctly stated that only those that can go through the narrow gate can enter into the kingdom of heaven. Without a true understanding of what it means a personal rapture cannot and will not take place.

So, while there are many that are waiting for that "beam me up Scottie" moment for a new Noah to build an Ark, what is needed now is an understanding of the individual journey to the kingdom and the ability of the individual to seek and receive the peace they seek right here, right now. In Luke 17:20-23, it tells you that the kingdom of God is within and around you. It is up to you and your actions as to whether you are free enough of your baggage to enter into it.

Without a considerable knowledge of physics, science, and mathematics it is hard for a biblical scholar without the use of these modalities to perceive the wonders of the universal complexities and as well as the vastness of a single atom. The lack of such comprehension has led historians to write about everything in the simplest of statements, leaving nothing for the imagination to explore outside of one's limited personal relationships and societal morays.

So many seekers of the Light sit and wait for signs from heaven that rapture is eminent or soon coming; for any sign would be a hopeful sign in a world gone so long without hope.

Observations of the Duality found in the bible

Before there was an earth realm, all was spirit and all was within the kingdom of the Most High God.

The Archangel Michael as we call angels of rank saved the spiritual kingdom from the invasion of erroneous thought forms. Those who were corrupted where relegated to the lower realms and cut off from the higher spiritual realms. This was not an instantaneous occurrence, it happened over a long period of time. With many a back and forth soul searching, and pleas for changing course, but eventually a separation came about with the first or real exodus.

The parting of the primeval waters or the void that separated the heavens from the earthly realm, the portal between the realms, whatever you want to call it, happened and those who chose to leave did so with the understanding that it was their choice; their free will, and that the portal would forever be closed to them and that travel between the two realms would be forever cut off from them.

The saying that you must be able to go through the eye of the needle in order to go through the narrow gate became a reality for those that had taken the erroneous thought forms into their being and had lost their spiritual protection.

The nakedness of Adam and Eve is depicted in the bible, but the truth is that it is really referencing what happened to the children once they lost their spiritual protection, they were left naked, unprotected, and vulnerable to the elements of their new existence.

Prior to this time, all was spirit and all was one, and all was of a single origin and a single mind.

This was the introduction of the sin nature in the children of God. It is important to point out here that the bible clearly states that no more than somewhere between a third or fourth of the children fell victim to the great deception. Therefore, it is fair to say that all were not subject to a sin nature. So when you hear "we have all sinned and fallen short..." you can now know that this was never true, for some fought and resisted the sin of betrayal and received the immortal inheritance of everlasting life or immortality.

We will never know how many thousands or millions of years everything took, for us to go from the highest form of intelligence we could imagine to a base primitive life form, in just the difference between Genesis chapter one and Genesis chapter two.

We will never know how long the portal between the heavenly realm and the earthly realm was freely open, but there is evidence all over the world that it lasted for a long duration of time and left evidence all over the globe.

The historians tried to amalgamate the massive span of history into a few thousand years finally by dividing it into two separate timeframes called pre-history and history. This, of course, did a great disservice to everyone without a hidden agenda.

The bible which is supposed to give us a blueprint on how to live a worthy life as a child of the Most High God, were never even told to only bow to the Most High God and as such have bowed their heads and bent their knees to many false little gods along the way, until many have completely lost their way. The saying, "my people perish for lack of knowledge..." is so true.

I have always wondered by Egypt with its entire splendor and grandeur got such a bad rap in the biblical story and was featured so prominently in the exodus story. Now this is what I think it truly represented.

Egypt represented the splendor of the heavenly realm the time where everything was created by thought, not by manual labor. The exodus and the passages in the story of the Garden of Eden intersect here become of the passages of man having to work the land and woman having to painfully bear children. Simply meaning life outside of the Heavenly realm (Egypt) would be hard.

This is evident right from the beginning in Genesis chapter two. It is also told in the Book of Exodus where it states that the only food they had was the food they received from heaven. Which leads to another knowing that the heavenly realm could always come down, but the earthly realm could not go up.

Stories are told in the physical realm as if that is exactly where they occurred but it is the retelling of an old truth from before the beginning of time as we know it. A story with so many modifications, that you might wonder if even God would recognize it.

There was a need to create an earthly Christ for there was a heavenly Christ, but if you cannot do it exactly, it is false. Just as the golden calf was not a true representation of the Most High God, neither can a child born of a woman still have the distinction of being without genealogy; without mother and father, immortal and a priest forever. Yet, it deems important that an earthly Christ had to come to save those because they were all born in sin and only a savior could save them and assure that the gates of heaven would open wide and receive them.

Someone sold this bill of good because, the people had grown lazy and lacked the gifts of the Holy Spirits and didn't want to work for them. So savior was created to give them hope, that even in their greediest state they would still be able to just ask for forgiveness and receive access to the kingdom of heaven again.

While at the same time denying others that say they are sorry, pardons from the prisons built to put them in for stealing food to feed their children, or for not being able to pay the adsorbent interest rates, they charged the less fortunate.

Yes, the earth needed a savior to save them because they unfortunately could not sufficiently change their ways enough to go through the eye of the needle or travel through the narrow gate which was a requirement of the Most High God.

So while both messages were preached, which one do you think was the most likely to get accepted first?

The only problem is that is there is a line in the bible that gets overlooked and it is, "not one jot or tittle will change until heaven and earth shall pass away." Therefore no matter how many earths pass away, until heaven itself also passes away, whatever was decreed from the beginning remains fully in effect. You cannot change the logos of the Most High God, to suit any earthly purpose.

The same is true with priesthoods. The Most High God said Melchizedek was a priest forever. Yet the bible managed to not only recognize the priesthood of Melchizedek, but also decided to create the priesthood of the Levi's and then the priesthood of Aaron. God actually had nothing to do with the creation of either.

The Most High God had a covenant with the children of single origin, the off-springs of Abraim and Sari, but the bible chose to change their names Abraham and Sarah an precede to create another covenant that suited their needs better. None is this was in accordance with the will of the Most High God.

I am grateful to the bible because the one sure way to read the bible is with spiritual armor, when cloaked in the spirit the Thoughtland is accessible and even the fogeyish verse can be seen in the clearest light.

The bible is alive and well when you ask for truth and are willing to have eyes to see and ears to hear.

Definition: Sealed

Ephesians 1:13 (KJV)
In whom ye also trusted, after that ye heard the word of truth, the gospel of your
*salvation: in whom also after that ye believed, ye were **sealed** with that Holy*
Spirit of promise,

Ephesians 1:11
*In whom also we have obtained an **inheritance**, being predestinated according to*
the purpose of him who worketh all things after the counsel of his own will:

      Those who were predestined before the foundation of the earth
were indeed sealed for they had obtained an inheritance that others that
came after them did not receive, and that was unconditional acceptance of
the Most High God.
These were the Children of the Most High God; they were the chosen, the
elected, and the sealed. They were given eternal and everlasting life.
      What is really important about Ephesians is that it talks of the time
before time began. It talks of the period before Genesis' "in the
beginning". The period where all was spirit and flesh had not come into
being.

Ephesians 4:30
And grieve not the Holy Spirit of God, whereby ye are sealed unto the day of
redemption.

      I feel that this verse has been wrongly interpreted by the ancient
scholars solely based on a literal interpretation. For when trying to put
some ancient knowing into an everyday life context one draws from what
one believes and/or has experienced, which may or may not be factual.

What was the purpose of the seal?

      For those that were a part of the divine design of the plan of the
Most High God, whose steps have been ordered and whose life has
meaning and purpose, they were with the Most High God before the
foundation of the world. The bible said that every hair on their head was
known.
      The seal was the Most High God's way of keeping the purity of the
Children of the Most High God free from admixture in the lower realms.
The is no way of knowing exactly when they were sealed, was it at the
beginning, or was it at the time of the upheaval in the heavens? When you

go over the time leading up to the great exodus story, you find that every door that had the blood mark on it was bypassed, this was like a seal, and it too was during a time of great upheaval, so it makes sense that the children were sealed for their protection from the future.

What does it mean and who has the power to do it and if they have the power to do it can they undo it?

Only by the power of the Most High God could this be accomplished and what is done cannot be undone until Heaven and Earth shall pass away.

In Ephesians, it is said that the author of the book was speaking about and to the faithful, the saints, and the holy ones.   Therefore, by inference it is setting them apart from the rest, who are not faithful, saints, or holy ones; which then brings credence to them being born into the time before time; in the world without form, or in this case a body without form.

Who and when were the sealed chosen?

Ephesians 1:4
According as he hath chosen us in him before the foundation of the world, that we should be holy and without blame before him in love:

Only the Most High God could have chosen us before the foundation of the world, because the Most High God is our creator, but more importantly is the timing of our creation.

Ephesians 1:5
Having predestinated us unto the adoption of children by Jesus Christ to himself, according to the good pleasure of his will,

We were predestined before the foundation of the world.

Ephesians 1:9
Having made known unto us the mystery of his will, according to his good pleasure which he hath purposed in himself:

Instilled in us is the mystery of the will of the Most High God.

Ephesians 1:10
That in the dispensation of the fullness of times he might gather together in one all things in Christ, both which are in heaven, and which are on earth; even in him:

Sealed so that at the fullness of time (end) we can recalled to heaven, identified as the Children of the Most High God being called home.

Ephesians 1:11, 17-18
In whom also we have obtained an inheritance, being predestinated according to
the purpose of him who worketh all things after the counsel of his own will:
That the God of our Lord Jesus Christ, the Father of glory, may give unto you the
spirit of wisdom and revelation in the knowledge of him:
The eyes of your understanding being enlightened; that ye may know what is the
hope of his calling, and what the riches of the glory of his inheritance in the saints,

For we have been promised an inheritance.

Ephesians 1:21
Far above all principality, and power, and might, and dominion, and every name
that is named, not only in this world, but also in that which is to come:

The inheritance is greater than mere earth alone but extends to everything beyond Earth.

Ephesians 2:8
For by grace are ye saved through faith; and that not of yourselves: it is the gift of
God:

The Children of the Most High God were saved through grace which will be everlasting, not by any works of their hand. It was a gift from the Most High God.

Definition: New Wine in Old Skins

Matthew 9:17 (KJV)
Neither do men put new wine into old wineskins {bottles}; else
the wineskins {bottles} break, and the wine runneth out, and
the wineskins {bottles} perish; but they put new wine into new wineskins {bottles},
and both are preserved

This is important because there were two set of principles on the earth plane and they found it hard to get the ancients to come around to the new way of thinking. This went way back long before the time of the Christ of the Roman Empire times. This was from the beginning when there were clearly two camps of people on the earth plane. There were

---

those that believed in the Most High God and those that believed in the LORD.

The teachings of both bore nothing in common and hence the statement. Today we just say, "You can't teach and old dog new tricks!", but in this case, it's more like you can't fool someone that already knows the truth.

The Biblical Creation of Fear

At some time in our thinking we are called upon to consider the masculine nature of the earthly realm.

Lord is a masculine title.

The earth age after the flood was under a masculine influence which replaced the influence of the Heavenly Holy Spirit.
On earth you had:
- LORDS
- Lords
- gods
- Kings
- Princes

These were the titles given to your new leaders, and the list of titles only grew as new additional masculine leader emerged. Each rebellion gave power to new leaders; each conquest of land brought others into servitude and the rise of masculine might and force reigned supreme on the vast majority of the earthly plane.

A rebellion between might and right is a repeated theme throughout the ages, as right struggles to remain relevant from the beginning to now.

It was the rebellion from the beginning that necessitated the creation of fear.

The story of Sodom and Gomorrah is for me at the center of its creation.

Even before I got to the Sodom and Gomorrah story in the bible, there were bells and whistles going off at the very mention of Lot leaving with Sari and Abriam. For some reason which was not clear to me at the time, Lot seemed really out of order, and in the wrong place. He just didn't fit into the narrative as he was supposed to fit.

By this time I had become accustomed to the flags that offered more questions than answers, so yet another question was placed on the shelf in my brain. Lot was indeed a puzzle that continued to nag at me from time to time.

I had already learned to think that nothing of the literal interpretation of the bible was gospel, so my mind kept being inquisitive about Lot and later even more so with his connection to Sodom and Gomorrah.

Two's are very important and prominent in the bible which made it very odd to have Sari and Abraim, being told by the High Priest Melchizedek that they would leave the Garden of Eden and become the parents of many nations, only to have them go off with Lot. It is important to notice that the High Priest did not mention Lot or what his role would be in nation building. Here they were going off into a strange land and we are left clueless as to who this person is or why he was chosen. This was a major biblical event and to this day historians still cannot get the relationship between Abraim and Lot straight, some say it is his brother, while other say he is his nephew or cousin, I err of the side of the place holder.

Just as the two's are an important number in the bible, three is a very important number in the bible and Lot, Sodom and Gomorrah do not a trinity make, for three was strictly reserved for the purpose of the Trinity. Since the bible's foundation is built on symbolism, it placed Lot once again out of order.

All of these questions came about before I had the insight of the *Thoughtland* at my disposal.

The bible itself was written on seven different levels that I could think of and maybe more, so looking strictly at the meaning of Lot's name gave meaning and understanding as to why the placement of Lot with Abraim and Sari was important to be there.

Lot means veil or covering, in the bible it is the veil that separates on from God just as it does in the symbolic representation of the inner structure of the Ark of the Covenant.

Therefore, by placing Lot behind Sari and Abraim as they left the Garden of Eden, Lot represented not a person but the veil of separation between God and those who rebelled in some way against the heavenly realms.

I also want to point out that it is quite telling that because of the All Seeing Eye, Melchizedek was able to relay their future of being the parents of many nations.

It is also clear why the bible tells Abraim that he will be the father of many nations, I always include Sari as a parent, even though the bible does not. There are a few facts still just out of view, which may become clear later.

There are two additional things about Lot's appearance that are really noteworthy. First there is the destruction of Sodom and Gomorrah a city filled with sin and Homosexual acts and lazy greedy women according to the biblical stories.

Are we to believe that these two things were enough for "God" to bring destruction to an entire city? In what religion is it ever possible to place God in such an unloving vengeful demeanor?

If God could do this then surely The Christ would have done it as well. Surely he would have shown no mercy on those that whipped him, pierced his sides, stripped him of his clothes, gambled to see who would win them, or those that gave him bitter herbs to drink, or placed thorns on his head, surely they would have had the wrath of God rain down on them in an instant. Isn't that what vengeful gods do?

The second important Lot connected story is the symbolism of Lot seeing his wife turned into a pillar of salt which would have struck fear in anyone and did strike fear into all that longs to return to the heavenly realm and leave this earthly place that had not lived up to the hype.

By offering up Homosexuality and lazy greedy women as reasons for the downfall of Sodom and Gomorrah, it was then the same as it is today a very convenient scapegoat.

The actors behind the scenes the Lords, Kings and clergy all conspired to instill *fear* and as control mechanism while at the same time laying blame squarely at the feet of others.

I keep sensing a certain willingness to blame women in the bible for all the woes, wrongs, and downfalls of man, with absolutely no regard for their part in bring themselves down. Why is it always a cry of "she did it to poor little me" being uttered by some burly built, sword carrying man?

I think Lot's wife real or imagined for the sake of the story was sorry that she ever listen and left heaven and that she was symbolic of so many that when on journey that they now is one of no return.

The ultimate weapon *fear* is one that keeps you in a self-imposed prison. But what is the motivator that makes us do it, why it's called Hell. Hell is that place, were fire and brimstone lives, and where it is groundhog day every day. No one wants to go there, so we try desperately to follow the thousands of do's and don'ts of the church, as well as the thousands heaped on us by the central government, only manage to live in fear because it is only a matter of time when either the church or the government will find of us quality of something.

Judgment Day becomes a very scary proposition, which has some opting for the "live now and die young" attitude because they don't see a way out of the incarceration of the mind.

Hell was sold to us as a real place. It was called many things in the bible from a lake of fire, to Sheol, Hades, Tartarus, and Gehenna. There are several bibles that list the word "Hell" numerous times.

The Latin Vulgate 110 and all of the King James Versions from 54 to 32 times, Holman Christian Standard Bible, while some others do not mention it at all, such as Young's, Twentieth Century New testament, Rotherham's Emphasized Bible, Weymouth's Testament, Jewish Publication Society Bible OT, Emphatic Dialott Greek/English Int. or the Tamakh The Complete Jewish Bible.

Hell seems to have a very special place in the western bibles and in their teachings. It also seems to leave very little wiggle room for the sinners or the trying. But it is not "Hell" that should be the bad rap, it is just a mind construct that we the people have adopted as our own personal bottomless pit, that any second might swallow us up.

The creation of fear is firmly embedded in our lives. There are triggers everywhere, we are afraid of just about everything today:

- The air we breathe is poisonous with pollutants from Chemtrails
- The water is polluted with poisons, garbage, sharks, and now alligators
- The people of different colors are taking your food, water, jobs and they've come the rob, rape and kill you
- The government is ripping you off
- Wall Street is ripping you off
- Main Street is ripping you off
- Your representative are ripping you off

But did you ever notice, no ever says your church is ripping you off, or that they are not giving you the whole truth and nothing but the whole truth? Or that their responsibility to teach you to have a personal relationship to the Most High God, is not being done?

Traveling into Genesis to review the foundation of the beginning

Chapter Five

The Book of Genesis

*G*enesis: The foundational Book of the bible requires explanation

This is true according to all Christian biblical literature, there is no other place to start, but in Genesis.

In Genesis 1:26-31(KJV) we see that humankind was created on the sixth day.

And God said, "Let us make man in our image, after our likeness: and let them have dominion over the fish of the sea, and over the fowl of the air, and over the cattle, and over all the earth, and over every creeping thing that creepeth upon the earth."

So God created man in his own image, in the image of God created he him; male and female created he them.

And God blessed them, and God said unto them, Be fruitful, and multiply, and replenish the earth, and subdue it: and have dominion over the fish of the sea, and over the fowl of the air, and over every living thing that moveth upon the earth.

And God said, Behold, I have given you every herb bearing seed, which is upon the face of all the earth, and every tree, in the which is the fruit of a tree yielding seed; to you it shall be for meat.

And to every beast of the earth, and to every fowl of the air, and to everything that creepeth upon the earth, wherein there is life, I have given every green herb for meat: and it was so.

And God saw everything that he had made, and, behold, it was very good. And the evening and the morning were the sixth day

God rested on the seventh day in Genesis 2:1-3

Thus the heavens and the earth were finished, and all the host of them.

And on the seventh day God ended his work which he had made; and he rested on the seventh day from all his work which he had made.

And God blessed the seventh day, and sanctified it: because that in it he had rested from all his work which God created and made.

Then in Genesis 2:4, we have the introduction of the LORD God into the language of whom we regularly pray. But this is not the same as the God of our creation, but the LORD of the "fall".

Genesis 2:4-6

These are the generations of the heavens and of the earth when they were created, in the day that the LORD God made the earth and the heavens,
⁵ And every plant of the field before it was in the earth, and every herb of the field before it grew: for the LORD God had not caused it to rain upon the earth, and there was not a man to till the ground.
⁶ But there went up a mist from the earth, and watered the whole face of the ground.

These cannot be the generations of the Heavens, because no living creature knows anything about what went into the making of heaven, or the creation of all there is in the heavens above. It does seem to quite nicely point out that there are two very different perspectives on the creation of the earth story, and it sounds as if it is told by two in two very different timeframes.

Now with my eyes wide open, I would be hard pressed to take anything I read on face value.

In Genesis2:7-8, The LORD it seems decides to make a mankind of his own and formed man of the dust of the ground and breathed into his nostrils, the breath of life and man became a living soul.

Now what boggles the mind and causes the brain to overload is that it is plain to see that there are two separate types of beings mentioned in the book of Genesis. Information I was never made aware of in any bible study class I had ever taken from any scholarly clergy, layperson, or seminary writer of Western biblical commentaries.

Genesis 3:22-24

And the LORD God said, Behold, the man is become as one of us, to know good and evil: and now, lest he put forth his hand, and take also of the tree of life, and eat, and live
for ever:
Therefore the LORD God sent him forth from the garden of Eden, to till the ground from whence he was taken.

Do you see this? The LORD God sent him out of the garden to till the ground from whence he was taken.

Again we see the two different creation stories and how one binds everything to the earth, dust, ground and the other simply states, *"let us make man in our image after our likeness..."* in a time before time began and which continued until heaven and earth were disconnected.

Genesis 3:24
So he drove out the man; and he placed at the east of the garden of Eden Cherubims, and a flaming sword which turned every way, to keep the way of the tree of life.

Now this sound more like what the Most High God did to the children of the fall than what is said to have happened to the Children of the Most High God. It may be that stories are so being intertwined into a new fabric that we can't pick them apart.

In verse 22 it stated, *"lest he put forth his hand, and take also of the tree of life, and eat, and live forever:"*

It looks like the Most High God wasn't concerned with the knowledge of good and evil, but the obtaining of everlasting life. Therefore, even in heaven there was a time when not all beings were created equal. Very interesting isn't it, to think that this in a shift in everything we have been taught?

Here it seems to suggest, that there was indeed a heavenly Garden of Eden before the earthy one. It also suggests that Genesis chapter 3 is out of order because verse 24 clearly speaks of the cut-off of the heavenly realms by the Cherubims from those kicked out of heaven.

Genesis 6:1-2
And it came to pass, when men began to multiply on the face of the earth, and daughters were born unto them,
That the sons of God saw the daughters of men that they were fair; and they took them wives of all whom they chose.

Here you can see for yourself when and where the two different beings on the earth converged. This was before the heavens and the earth were separated and guarded by the Cherubim.

Genesis 6:13-14
*And God said unto Noah, The end of all flesh is come before **Me**; for the earth is filled with violence through them; and, behold, I will destroy them with the earth. Make thee an ark...*

It probably stands to reason, that to separate the heavens above from the ground below, after enjoying a period of no separation between the two was an earth shattering event. It would indeed be expected to cause such a catastrophic event in history; it would be recorded and orally passed down. But, of course, by the time it reached 2,000 years ago all the names, dates, places and reasons had long been changed to denote their understanding of what seemed possible in their era. No matter how illogical it sounds, or how after 2,000 years of trying to fact check historical events, in order to prove them, it still has not been done.

The bible recorded two major water events

The Great Flood and the reason for building Noah's Ark, and the parting of the Red sea which opened up to let the great exodus out of Egypt. Which, after fleeing the Egypt army and successfully crossing into the promised land, the Red sea closed up killing the Egyptian army.

In both scenarios, because there was enough water to drown everyone, it made it a phenomenal occurrence in the bible.

Also, in each instance there was a recording of livestock, water and livestock, danger and upheaval, vengeance and raft, and a need for a change. And let us not forget the constant references to forty days, forty generations, or 40 years also recorded as gestation periods, which I now see as correction periods, that in the Exodus story, it as much, as says so, in not so subtle ways.

Those who took the exodus from the heavenly realm who wanted to go to the earthly Garden of Eden were barred from entry into the "promised land" for 40 years. Forget everything you have read about this on a literal level, this was all done on a spiritual level by the mastermind of the spiritual plane.

They were contaminated and had to be cleansed of the impurities of their hearts.

Exodus Chapter 16:1-4
And they took their journey from Elim, and all the congregation of the children of Israel came unto the wilderness of Sin, which is between Elim and Sinai, on the fifteenth day of the second month after their departing out of the land of Egypt.
² And the whole congregation of the children of Israel murmured against Moses and Aaron in the wilderness:
³ And the children of Israel said unto them, Would to God we had died by the hand of the LORD in the land of Egypt, when we sat by the flesh pots, and when we did eat bread to the full; for ye have brought us forth into this wilderness, to kill this whole assembly with hunger.
⁴ Then said the LORD unto Moses, Behold, I will rain bread from heaven for you; and the people shall go out and gather a certain rate every day, that I may prove them, whether they will walk in my law, or no.

We will never know if it was 40 years, 400 years or 40 million years, for all time was an is an earthly construct and certainly of no consequence to the ALL. But Exodus 16:1 states clearly for those that have eyes to see that the children of Israel came unto the wilderness of Sin. I think that it is very important not to take this on face value alone, and not to think of it as just a place in the bible, but to see it as a condition of the origin of the sin nature, and the real reason for the need to wonder in the wilderness for a complete gestation period.

A Review of Psalms for clarification Purposes

Chapter Six

The Psalms –
My search for the Most High God

All of my research was found in the King James Version of the Holy Bible. It was the chosen bible of my mother's faith.
The Psalms were my comfort in all times of trouble as well as my security blanket in good times. I wore the Psalms as a protective covering throughout my entire life. My mother taught me to love the psalms as a little child and I never departed from them.   My granddaughter could recite the 23rd Psalm when she was just two years old. The 23rd was my favorite. You could feel the love of the comfort of the Most High for her children, in their time of need streaming from this psalm.

It was a great shock to me, that my comfort level with the psalm would be shaken to its core, when I asked that simple question about Genesis chapter two, when the title "LORD" first showed up. In my mind it was not supposed to be there, because I had never noticed it before, thank you *Thoughtland*.

When had the Most High become a shepherd and when had we become sheep? This was not first age language, but was more like the language of the Christian era, only, the psalms were in the Old Testament, not in the Christian era at all.

My brain worked all night and wouldn't let me sleep. I woke up angry because I felt duped, deceived, compromised in some way. My worship had been to call upon the LORD in my favorite prayers, the 23rd Psalm and the LORD'S Prayer. I did so in earnest and in all sincerity, and always felt that my prayers were answered, and my connection to God was secure.

What I didn't know, for most of my life was, just how important the vibration of each word sent into the atmosphere is, and how each word carries with it a meaning separate and apart from just the word itself. I also had no knowledge at that time that there were different entities masquerading as the Alpha and the Omega were out there.

To my amazement, I had called upon, and I put my energy into asking, an entity to be my salvation; by simply calling on the LORD, instead of the Most High God.

Hallelujah, hallelujah, hallelujah, my eyes are open and can't be closed again. Even though old habits are hard to break my intentions are clear, and my mind knows that perhaps all I need to do is restore the psalm I love so much to its original intent. "The Most High is my Creator, I shall not want..." Suddenly my soul felt a measurement of peace and a feeling of home. I would rest well tonight.

"In the beginning was the Word and the Word was with God and the Word was God." An entire knowing is wrapped up in these words which I will explore later. But for now, in   Genesis Chapter One, we see that the good book tells us that everything was with God.

However in Genesis Chapter Two everything was according to the LORD, which is quite a shift from the Absolute wouldn't you say?

How had I missed it? Then upon realizing how many interchangeable references about and of God have been used over the many centuries, I was no longer surprised or as hard on myself as I was at the first knowing. I was also not surprised at just how little we do know, and just how few questions we ask, or allow our children and our children's children to ask. We have become the rote generations, we are the sheep, and we wonder why our children do drugs and why they distrust authority. What are they supposed to do when things don't make sense and don't fit together? We have not allowed our children to grow spiritually through the knowledge of knowing their true selves and who their true Creator is and will always be.

Our children are reacting to a world that is out of order while we continue to look at them as if they are out of order. If we decide to tackle the problems that has screwed up the world, that have changed the energy; if we lift the vibrational levels by replacing the negative energy with positive energy; if we don't just talk the talk while leaving the mechanisms in place that fuel the negative engine of this planet, we will have a chance to save our children's future by opening a path back to source.

The Psalms was like a testing ground for testing the substitutions of the ever evolving God vs. LORD theory.

When God was not the first reference in my favorite psalm, I decided to go through all 150 psalms to see how the titles were used and to see what I could learn. It turned out to be a big eye opener.

My study of the bible started at home with my mother, then onto church and Sunday school, midweek bible study, teaching youth Sunday school, taking the Universal Ministries Ordination Certification course and finally teaching the Metaphysical Universal Ministry course. Still I had not made the connection and at any point along the way, and no one else had either, to my knowledge.

So, are these two titles so alike, that it makes no different which one is used? Does the interchange of these two titles do little or nothing to change the vibration in the universe? Will the sound create exactly the same sound in the vibrational field of the universe?

To get an answer we must first look at the definitions of each word carefully to decide just on face value if their meanings are the same.

The dictionary says that *God* (in Christianity and other monotheistic religions) is the creator and ruler of the universe and the source of all moral authority; the Supreme Being; a being conceived as the perfect, omnipotent, omniscient originator and ruler of the universe.

The dictionary also says the Lord is a synonym for God. The dictionary describes LORD as someone or something having power, authority, or influence; a master or ruler.

The dictionary also says that God is a synonym for LORD.

But we don't have to stay confused because each letter contains its own separate relationship with the universe and each combination of letters denotes a distinct vibrational definition to the universe.

If, at the beginning the Word was LORD GOD, then maybe I could have bought it, but that is not what it said and the definitions of the two words further prove why it was not so.

By its very definition a LORD has no creative power, there is nothing omnipotent or omniscient about someone who is given an earthly title, for any title taken or bestowed can just as easily be taken away.

Let's look at how the 150 psalm describe the two titles, and how they have shifted throughout the psalms, that the biblical scholars would have us to believe where written by one Psalter. Even though, the varying tones and degrees of the Psalter's grief, joy, elation and sorrow were disconcerting over the years, I never questioned any of it until now.

The breakdown of the psalms:

Verses 1 – 21
The LORD was referenced 20 times
God was referenced 11 times

Verses 22 – 48
The LORD was referenced 22 times
God was referenced 17 times

Verses 49 – 78
The LORD was referenced 16 times
God was referenced 30 times

Verses 79 – 106
The LORD was referenced 27 times
God was referenced 18 times
LORD God was referenced 7 times

Verses 107 – 150
The LORD was referenced 44 times
God was referenced 11 times
Other references
LORD our God – 3
Oh God, The LORD – 1
LORD his God – 1
Where God is the LORD – 1
God of Jacob – 1

All of this stands to prove that if all of this was indeed written by one person, we would be fools to believe anything coming from a person that couldn't keep the name of the his Most High straight in his head from one verse to another.
Just when I would think to myself, it is all just circumstantial evidence, and the verdict could go either way depending on how one chose to look at it; just when I thought the jury is still out, and I could be found wrong on every count; I would receive not just a flicker, or a glimmer of light, but a floodlight would go on.
I think these psalms will speak to you as they did to me. I think they will cause you to see with new eyes things that may never have been seen before, and may cause you to have thoughts you may never have thought before.

Psalm 37:9
For evildoers shall be cut off; but those that wait upon the LORD, they shall inherit the earth.

It is only when you begin to see as I did the significance of the difference between Genesis Chapter One and Genesis Chapter Two, that a verse in Psalms takes on a whole different meaning and can validate your new found understanding and assumptions.
For Children of the Most High God do not stand to inherit the earth, for everything on the earth plane will die, but their inheritance was received before the foundation of the world began and it is immortality and utterly unworldly.
They know or will be awakened to the fact that this is not their home and that this is not a place to aspire to own, but a place to run from.

The devil is in the details. The LORD that promises you the earth is the very one that created the division between Heaven and Earth in the first place. This LORD has no intention of and no desire to let you ever leave his kingdom.
Remember ashes to ashes and dust to dust? It is important to know the difference.

Psalm 37:11
But the meek shall inherit the earth; and shall delight themselves in the abundance of peace

Remember render unto Caesar what is Caesar's and unto God's what is Gods'?
The earth belongs to Caesar and Caesar has no intention of giving it to you. But the bigger truth is that all that Caesar has is a mere drop in the bucket compared to the vastness of the universes of the Most High God, who has given you an inheritance.

Although everything has become twisted, now is the time, before time runs out, for us to unravel it all and see the whole truth.

Psalm 50:1
The mighty God, even the LORD hath spoken, and called the earth from the rising of the sun unto the going down thereof

Here is the proof I was looking for and I had searched all over, that even the bible has recorded that God and the LORD are different entities. This verse seems to suggest that the two decided that there would be a split between the heavens and the earth.

Psalm 52:8-9
But I am like a green olive tree in the house of God: I trust in the mercy of God forever and ever I will praise thee forever: And I will wait on thy name; for it is good before thy saints.

It is good to wait; it is good to pray. But it is of utmost importance to know to whom you are praying and on whom you are waiting. There are little gods and masters, kings and LORDS out there, but there is only one Most High God, the Alpha and Omega; the ALL.

Psalm 53:2-3
God looked down from heaven upon the children of men to see if there were any that did understand, that did seek God. Every one of them is gone back, they are altogether become filthy; there is none that doeth good not one.

This is so very important to know, we are not children of men, we are the children of the Most High God, we are sealed and our salvation is never in question. We will sojourn here for a little while, but we are not from here, and will not be here forever.

Psalm 54:3-4
For strangers are risen up against me, and oppressors seek after my soul: they have not set God before them. Behold, God is mine helper: The LORD is with them that uphold my soul.

For a book that is supposed to bring us a roadmap, a blueprint to salvation, I have to ask, can it get any more confusing?

Psalm 55:9
Destroy, O LORD, and divide their tongues; for I have seen violence and strife in the city.

So we are supposed to ask the LORD to destroy, seek vengeance? This is not something anyone would ask of a loving benevolent God, a master yes, one in authority over the city yes, but never the Most High God.

Psalm 55:16
And as for me, I will call upon God; and the LORD shall save me.

This is a veiled attempt to make God and the LORD seem like they are the same, when clearly we can see that the energies of the two are definitely different in every way. There is a burning question here. Why?

Psalm 58:1-4
Do you indeed speak righteousness, you silent ones? Do you judge uprightly, you sons of men? No, in heart you work wickedness; you weigh out the violence of your hands in the earth.
The wicked are estranged from the womb; They go astray as soon as they are born, speaking lies.
Their poison is like the poison of a serpent;

When the bible speaks of the sons of men, it is referring to Genesis Chapter Two when the LORD not God said let us make man in our image. These are their children. The womb is of the Mother and the Mother is in the Heavens, they are indeed estranged for they know her not. Whereas, the Children of the Most High can never be estranged from their Mother; she knows every hair on their head as spoken of in Ephesians. Although you reside here on earth, you are forever linked to and preserved for the Most High God.

Psalm 59:16-17
But I will sing of thy power; yea, I will sing aloud of thy mercy in the morning; for thou hast been my defense and refuge in the day of my trouble. Unto thee, O my strength, will I sing: for God is my defense and the God of my mercy.

This sounds like the pray you would expect from a child of the Most High God. Notice the language, the tone and the hope in those words. My heart immediately responds. I feel the reverence and the knowing of what to expect from a parent and is required of a child. To them God is merciful, God is refuge, and of God one does not ask what is not in God nature to give.

Psalm 63:1
O God they are my God; early will I seek thee; my soul thirsteth for thee, my flesh longest for thee in a dry and thirsty land, where no water is.

The first six words are a full recognition, that there are other gods and deities afoot, and that one has to make it clear to who they are addressing. Why we weren't told about them is a travesty to say the least. The next very important finding for me was the acknowledgement that the earth has no living water. God is the living water and there is none on Earth. The third thing that was very telling was that the Children of the Most High long for their spiritual home which is not earth. This passage must have been from some really old ancient manuscripts, tablets or something, because at this particular point in time there was a genuine knowing that seems to be lost today. It also makes a reference to the earth of Genesis Chapter Two and the condition they found the earth in at that time.

Psalm 72:18
Blessed be the LORD God, the God of Israel who only does wondrous things.

This is the first time I am seeing the amalgamation of the two titles to refer to the God of earthly Israel. It is amazing how they can be two separate entities in one psalm and then the same in another, as if we couldn't get any more confused.

Psalm 76:1, 6, 11-12

In Judah is God known his name is great in Israel
At my rebuke O God of Jacob
Vow, and pay unto the LORD your God; Let all that be round about him bring presents unto him that ought to be feared
He shall cut off the spirit of princes: He is terrible to the kings of the earth

There is a real shift in the energies found in these verses. The rebuking is akin to a casting of a spell; the passages are full of vengeance, violence and fear and through it all he seeks presents as a reward. This seems to be a further sinking into the abyss of the earth realm and further and further away from heaven's grasp.

Psalm 77:9
Hath God forgotten to be gracious? Hath he in anger shut up his tender mercies?

It seems that at least someone working on the Psalms wasn't feeling the love either, for when they looked, they did not find them in all the psalms.

Psalm 136:1-6, 26
O give thanks unto the LORD; for he is good: for his mercy endureth for ever.
O give thanks unto the God of gods: for his mercy endureth for ever.
O give thanks to the Lord of lords: for his mercy endureth for ever.
To him who alone doeth great wonders: for his mercy endureth for ever.
To him that by wisdom made the heavens: for his mercy endureth for ever.
O give thanks unto the God of heaven: for his mercy endureth for ever.

It seems that much was known about all the many little gods that were floating around during those days, but we were never asked to clarify and become precise in our acknowledgement. But somehow in verse 26 they almost got it right, at lease pretty close. It seems they tried to include them all.

Psalm 137:4
How shall we sing the LORD'S song in a strange land?

This is an excellent question that the fallen must have asked once they realized that they were indeed in a strange land. For it is quite evident, that the earth was no longer the land that they thought it to be or would be or was. This leads me to think that maybe the flood of the Old Testament really happened as a way to separate the two realms.

The story of the parting of the red sea and leading the people out of Egypt and then having the waters swallow everyone else up. Maybe there is more to this story and maybe somehow it had a heavenly component that was fictionalized over time.

Psalm110:1
The LORD said unto my LORD sit thou at my right hand until I make thine enemies thy footstool.

Well, isn't this amazing? Who is talking to whom? This is the question: how many LORDS can there be at one time? I have no answer for this. Have eyes to see...

Gleanings from a few verses in the Books of Samuel

Chapter Seven

Books of Samuel - Pursuing the Search for The Most High God

1 Samuel 15:2-3 (KJV)
Thus said the LORD of hosts, I remember that which Amalek did to Israel, how he laid wait for him in the way when he came up from Egypt.
Now go and smite Amalek and utterly destroy all that they have and spare them not: but, slay, man and woman, infant and suckling, ox and sheep, camel and ass.

The sewing of seeds of vengeance in the bible and making it a normal way to react has allowed violence to become the natural way to handle every action and every reaction throughout our history as a human race, especially as it pertains to wants and desires.

1 Samuel 18:10
*And it came to pass on the morrow, that the **evil spirit from God** came upon Saul, and he prophesied in the midst of the house; and David played with his hand, as at other times and there was a javelin in Saul's hand.*

Now we are supposed to believe, without ever questioning, that there is an evil spirit coming from our God, and going into a human to make him think and do evil? This reminds me of the title of the play *"Children of a lesser god"*, for surely this is what it must be, a lesser god!

1 Samuel 19:9
And the evil spirit from the LORD was upon Saul, as he sat in his house with his javelin in his hand; and David played with his hand.
This denotes an understanding that I myself am unfamiliar with, but I found it profoundly telling of something just beyond my grasp. But this I do know, good and evil just like oil and water, do not mix. You cannot put old wine in new skins.

---

1 Samuel 19:20
*And Saul sent messengers to take David; and when they saw the company of the prophets prophesying, and Samuel standing as appointed over them the **Spirit of God** was upon the messengers of Saul and they also prophesied.*

Notice how clearly the two different and distinct entities with very different energies create different behaviors. In 1 Samuel (you can see that the bible uses lower case to denote the lesser for "evil spirit of the LORD", while in verse 20 the "Spirit of God" is capitalized to denote greater. While it is very affirming to me know, my foundation as a child was formed without this understanding. Our society as people was formed without this understanding. The bible is nuanced in its representations of the messages it presents.

2 Samuel 19:20
For thy servant doth know that I have sinned; therefore behold, I am come the first this day of all the house of Joseph to go down to meet my lord the king.

When I read this I thought how normal it sounds to say my lord the king, while not normal at all to hear my god the king. Why because God is God and never an earthly entity, while lords are earthly beings with an earthly title.

2 Samuel 3:39
And I am this day weak, though anointed king; and these men the sons of Zeruiah be too hard for me the LORD shall reward the doer of evil according to his wickedness.

It is hard to me to wrap my head and my heart around any verse that speaks of rewarding the doer of evil according to his wickedness. I noticed the word was not to punish but to reward. This has been explained away, time and time again, as how they spoke in those days, but it wasn't just how they spoke, it was also how they thought, and to whom they held in high esteem. Their LORD had a very different set of standards, as well as, a very different set of attributes.
If everything we know about God starts with a lie we are already doomed to repeat our mistakes.
All of the different names of the Most High God, by consequence, have deceived us into thinking that we can just make up or use any name that suits us, in any given moment, and it will be just fine.
Of course, that is exactly what the deceivers want you to believe and to do. It is their entry ticket into your sacred space; their way into

your inner sanctum. Once in, just like the early depiction of the serpent in the garden, they get into your psyche and become a part of your thinking process. They weave threads of truth with strains of lies into the fabric of your knowledge base, until you cannot see the difference or untangle one from the other. It all becomes normal; the new norm is what the bible based all of its information on and has continuously delivered it to us as absolute fact.

Entering into the World of the Divine Mother

The Glimpse

Just for a moment
There was a crack in the veil
And in that moment
I saw Her
I really saw Her
And I knew
I just knew!

Chapter Eight

The Feminine Influence or Infusion

If you can believe that the teacher comes when the student is ready, you then will understand how I was divinely guided to come to the conclusion, that the explanation of our creation left too much to be desired, and it all cried out for a closer look.

At a time when I was in a good job and had a great career path ahead of me, was welled liked by my colleagues and upper management, I was suddenly terminated in a stunning reversal of fortune.

In shock, I didn't know it at the time, but it was one of the best things that ever could have happened to me.

Looking back, I realize my spiritual projection was so limited where I was, that in order to grow in spirit, I needed to be moved to an environment conducive to spiritual learning.

The inner spirit was yearning, at the same time the outer spirit was coping with all of the mundane aspects of every day survival.

My job search opened a door for a job interview, for which I had no qualifications, but I did so anyway thinking it would help me to get experience with the interview process, since I had been with the same company for over twelve years. I was amazed at how quickly I moved through the interview process and made it through four interviews and received a job offer even though I insisted on an increase in their salary offer. I, of course, accepted. Within six months of being on the job, I found out that the entire operation was moving out of Connecticut to New Jersey and Pennsylvania. I chose to relocate.

This began my spiritual growth, for almost as soon I asked a question on spirituality someone would be there to either answer the question or direct my path.

I did not see how everything was falling into place at the time, but it was all by divine order.

My job was filled with people who were perfectly placed to help lead and guide me through the learning curve of the daily routine one faces as they learn on the job. They were there to help me through the tangles of the relocation process. Everything was all smoothed out by all of the earth angels working with me and on my behalf. It is really comforting to have this knowing now. I, of course, realized none of this at the time.

One of the things I always did since I was a little child, after a move, was to find a church and my move to Pennsylvania was no different. I met a young lady, and after talking to her about many spiritual things, she directed me to a small metaphysical church in the community, which had a teaching program she thought would be of interest to me.

It was there that I met my mentor, a spiritual enlightened human with a big heart and a head full of knowledge she was always willing to share. The fact that she took me under her wing was a dream come true and a milestone in my universal journey.

She taught me all she could and eventually made me her protégé and later turned the teaching of her books and courses over to me. I taught for many years with her there to continuously guide me and mentor me, until I could do it no longer.

Some of her many gifts to me included her most prized spiritual book collection which I treasure to this day.

It was sometime after her death, I realized, that although we had dug deep into the weeds, we had not dug down to the root, and until that was done, the pieces of everything we held dear would not truly fit the narrative of the doctrine being taught.

The premise of everything being taught today in the western hemisphere is based entirely on the Greek interpretation of history, and has thus been presented from a white patriarchal perspective.

I am not exactly sure when I began to see how many gaps there was in the narrative I was teaching, which was far more enlightening than anything else I had ever been taught, but there were certain things that continued to nag at me and cause me to search deeper and deeper for answers which continued to allude me, just as much as they continued to tug at me.

The Holy Spirit, the Star of David represented in blue and white, the world without form, and "in the beginning", these terms and phrases and so many more would not let me rest on the vast knowledge I had already received, for something was still missing, something big and I knew it. I just didn't know what until I really started to do a deep analysis of "As above, so below" from the Gnostics and from the bible Genesis 1:1, "In the beginning".

When nothing is taken at face value, you really start to have eyes to see and ears to hear.

The iconic Mother and Child

The Mother and Child were originally represented as the Most High God and the Children of the Light. But in the second earth age; the age of the masculine, it became the Mother and son and gradually was just the Son who had evolved into the All – the Father - the Son – the Holy Spirit and the mother was lost. The Great Mother was reduced to just being the vessel that gave birth through the Immaculate Conception story. Trying to re-create in the second earth age what occurred naturally in the heavenly beginnings is no small feat and not one that could be duplicated, therefore deception was indeed necessary.

The significance of "as above, so below" was so important to the architects of this world, that a great deal of time and energy was spent on trying to replicate every aspect of the first earth age.

I began thinking that the 2012 ending, by Hopi standards, had signified the beginning of the end of another earthly realm, and the start of the preparation for us to enter into the new age to come.

If this is true we are in the end times of the Eighth Day and the Ninth Day or whatever day, is approaching. What could we possibly expect of such a time?

There would not have been a need for it, if there was any end in sight to what we are experiencing now, but alas there isn't, so I thoroughly expect a correction and a new beginning. A beginning in which we will actually stop fighting and start getting along, in a world where money doesn't rule everything and right prevails over might. A world where kindness and giving become commonplace and a world where people open their eyes and see that they and their brothers and sisters are guardianship to the new earth they inhabit.

But, in order to evolve into this new earth, we must rethink the Iconic Mother and Child. We have been taught that the Mother and Child represents the Immaculate Conception born on the earth realm, but how could this be, for the Iconic Mother and Child is the originator of our origins before the foundation of the earth as referenced in Ephesians 1:4. The children have a mother, but no father figure making it truly an Immaculate Conception. The second earth age explains it as having a Heavenly Father entering a mortal woman, which would mean it still takes two, therefore meaning it not an Immaculate Conception at all, by its own definition.

So here we have it the introduction to the lost feminine spiritual energy in the bible, which was vanished from the bible story in the second earth age.

In a moment of clarity, today, I realized just how insidious was the need to negate the feminine from any reference in the Epistles of the bible.

In Ephesians 1:2 it states, *"Grace be to you, and peace, from God our Father, and from the Lord Jesus Christ."*

All of the references are masculine which is clearly in conflict with anatomy.

The Iconic Mother and Child are conspicuously absent in his acknowledgement as he references Grace, which is clearly an attribute of the Mother, but the verse fails to mention the Mother at all. And the failure continues throughout the Epistles. This all harkens back to the need for a masculine God; one of might over right, vengeance over compassion, which changes the energy of everything in the earthly realm.

In Ephesians 1:11 it states, *"In whom also we have obtained an inheritance, being predestined according to the purpose of him who worketh all things after the counsel of his own will."*

Ephesians was always one of my favorite books because in it I found myself, I understood myself and where I came from and to whom I belonged. I never saw this version as I read. I saw my Mother, I felt her love, I understood her promise, but during the course of writing this, my eyes were opened to what the world was actually seeing and for the first time the deception was really brought home. How could we ever connect to her, go back to her if we did not know to call on her, and emulate her? The Kings James Version of the bible has become an all-male God and Savior bible, no room in the Inn for the Mother and her Children.

o   How did we ever let this happen?

o   When did women abdicate the throne?

o   When will we be ready to take it back?

Our children, our earth, and our ascension depend on our willingness to fight for the Mother energy, we must become the avatars we were designed and destined to be. We are not Stepford wives; we are not Barbie Dolls; we are not Mistresses, we are part of the Great Mother, her energy flows through our veins and nourishes our souls. We are her connection to here, and to there and without our awakening, she cannot heal the planet and change its course from destruction to healing.

We must remember that the "LORD" destination in Genesis Chapter two was not a spiritual realm terminology but a worldly term to denote one who had power and control of your destiny.

My conclusion is that the insertion of masculine energy to usurp the place of the Mother was also done to validate the introduction of the God of Heaven as the "LORD" of Earth and the Savior of mankind as the new Holy Trinity of masculine energy. Well that's just too much testosterone, in hindsight, when you really stop to think about it.

How can anything so completely unbelievable exist in the bible and never be discussed by biblical scholars, or seen by me during all of the years, in which I revered the book of Ephesians? It is clearly an example of just how blind we are before we wake up, or how intuitively blissful we are until we are called into purpose.

A Tribute to the Iconic Mother

The 23rd Psalm
After being raised on the 23rd Psalm, I could not forsake it.
The 23rd Psalm is what we turn to in times of a need for comfort, support and assurance that no matter where we walk we do not walk alone.
So why would I want to change it, I just want to make it mirror my new found understanding of the biblical instructions as I now perceive them.
Revised version of Psalm 23
The Most High God is my source; I shall not want.
She maketh me to lie down in green pastures: She leadeth me beside still waters.
She restoreth my soul: She leadeth me in the paths of righteousness for Her name's sake.
Yea, though I walk through the valley of the shadow of death I will fear no evil: for thou art with me; thy rod and thy staff they comfort me.
Thou preparest a table before me in the presence of mine enemies: thou anointeth my head with oil: my cup runneth over.
Surely goodness and mercy shall follow me all the days of my life and I will dwell in the house of the Most High God for ever.
By doing this I am putting my focus to the one true thing that is at the core of my re-knowing journey; a need to know and acknowledge the Mother-Creator-God of humankind as the eternal source of my strength.

The Returning Path

Everyone that is on this journey thinks it means they are moving forward,
When, in all actuality, being on this journey means moving backwards through
time
Until they reach they return to Source. The journey ends, when we return to
Where we began, and are one with the Source of our creation.
We will return to source and be "Whole and Absolute,"
Or we will return to the dirt!
As we are returning, our whole life will flash before our eyes, until we are back at
our beginnings.
Everyone thinks they will be heading toward the Light, and figuratively speaking
you are, but at the same time, you are moving further and further away from
everything, but the inside of the womb of the ALL.
And once inside you will find that in the darkness, you are the Light!
You are Home!
And you Re-know!

"The Light shines in the darkness and the darkness did not overcome it."
(John 1:5)

"Until the Lion learns how to write, every story will glorify the hunter."
- African Proverb

Chapter Nine

The Returning Path

It is 11-11-11

The time of 11-11-11 was supposed to be a wake-up call for everyone, so I looked at the world to see if I could pinpoint what might be a sign of what was to come, and I found it. Truth needed to be told. I had a truth to tell, I must not keep it to myself, but I continued to ponder how to begin.

The Master Number 11 is usually called 'the Illuminator', 'the Messenger' or 'the Teacher', as those under the influence of this Master Number are here to be inspirational guiding lights, and their mission is to bring illumination to others and to help raise spiritual awareness.

Number 11 is the number of trials, tests and treachery from others.

The Master Numbers possess more potential than other numbers. They are often highly charged, difficult to deal with and require time, maturity and great effort to integrate into one's personality. Master Number 11 people are very powerful and have volunteered to incarnate to help the human race. Their pathway is often hidden, and one must learn through experiences in both the outer and inner-worlds. Master Number 11 represents 'transformation'.

It is 12-12-12

Then came 12-12-12 and the end of the Mayan Calendar was upon us. Some had suggested that it meant the end of time, and preached doom and gloom, rapture and all sorts of unhappy ending.

Number 12 represents the educational process on all levels, the submission of the will required and the sacrifice necessary to achieve knowledge and wisdom on both Spiritual and Intellectual levels. When the intellect is sacrificed to the feelings, the mind will be illuminated with the answers it seeks. Attention paid to requirements of education will end suffering and bring success.

Nothing on the surface happened, but just beneath the surface a silent war was brewing, forces were aligning, and a clash of the Titians was almost certain. Dark verses Light, Good versus Evil, it became a time when random acts of violence became the norm and the new energies coming into our atmosphere were not agreeable to everyone on the earth. It seemed to cause a violent reaction in some, and unspeakable acts were and still are being committed.

They say it is the darkest before the dawn and I feel that we are at the dawn of a new age, and a clearing and a cleansing is about to take place. We will never know when it is finished or when it really began, but the signs are pointing to a need to be ever ready.

Why is there such a clash and why is it so important to us? It is important because we have been led astray and we do not know whose side we should be on and to whom we really belong.

In order to really be effective in the coming time, our eyes have to be opened and our mind has to be able to accept the things we will hear with ears that are opened to receive truth.

Thus, the truth about the Feminine is essential to our readiness and preparedness to be on the right side, just as we were asked at the beginning before time began to choose. We will be asked to choose again.

The Coming Shift in Thinking

In order to fully understand the Feminine, we must again return to the phrase "As above, so below" there is a running theme in Gnostic writings that bring this phrase front and center in so many instances. One cannot dismiss its true meaning and connection to everything. It applies to everything.

What we know for sure is that here on earth, all human creation come from the female human. Therefore, it is logical to conclude that the ability to create indeed enjoys the same concept in the heavens. Nothing came happen here that was not first conceived there, according to the Gnostics, but not so fast, because the saying "let us create…" human life (incidentally a much better terminology) in our image, didn't just originate in the heavens, but also was done in the earthly realm inhabited by the "fallen".

For The heavenly Feminine energy source did not need help, nor have a need to consult with any other beings, for within the Divine Feminine is, was, and forever will be total completeness. Just a single thought is all that is ever needed to create an entire universe, an entire planet, and especially human life.

Genesis 1:26 has to mean that the Feminine energy in the creation was our Mother and the symbol of the Child was US. There is no mention of a father anywhere in the verses, none, there is no mention at all. The verse might have read "let me make..." if a statement was ever needed at all, but in reality it was the creative power of the word that in energy terms was just a thought, for "thoughts are things and things have wings" another gift from the Gnostics.

In Genesis 1:3 God said, "'Let there be light', and there was light." No, "we", for no help was needed by the Omnipotent One!

The first humankind was complete in every aspect, needing nothing outside of itself to be whole and complete. And this is the proper meaning of when and how to use the statement, "as above, so below". It is not proper to use it out of context, because the intentions of the first earth age, which turned into the first earth realm, which was to create something that was in complete harmony with the Most High God.
It had the perfect union of the bride and groom, the unification of the Holy union of nothing missing, nothing broken, which is needed to perfectly create. The first humankind are thus the chosen ones and those who remained after the "fall" were sealed to keep their purity intact for all eternity as the Children of the Light.

The timing and the reason for the sealing is important because it does several things:
- Sealed the identify which would become important in the future
- Eliminates the ability to be tampered with as we see it happened in the future
- Insures that the inheritance was secured

We have acknowledged the Creator, without ever acknowledging the truth, which was staring us right in the face. Just think about it for a second. The Mother, The Holy Spirit, The Comforter are all attributes of the Feminine in heaven as it is to some degree on earth.
But this fundamental understanding is not a part of our present day understanding. It is not the normal way in which we address the God we serve.
So no, I don't think, "Let us make..." in Genesis 1:26, truly represents our creation or is in any way like what happened in Genesis Chapter 2.

The Mystery of the "Fallen"

The mystery surrounding "The Fallen" is essential to uncovering why there was such an obfuscation of the rightful Creator.

It is important to further state why the statement "...in our image..." is wrong and give further explanation as to why there was a fall from grace. There was a reason for the strife in heaven. It was hurt and a sense of loss and of pride in knowing that the Most High had created something with a characteristic of the nature of God that even the angels in heaven did not have. It was as if the first born had been displaced by the second born. The hurt was deep and profound and so unintended. The Most High had created the Angel kingdom but they were not created in her image, but humankind indeed was and this was another change that occurred in the bible to make us think that the angels and God had the same DNA, thus the same abilities and likeness.

Why was there jealousy between humankind and angels?

What was the big difference between humankind and angels?

The angels were created first but they were not created in the Likeness and image of the Most High God, for humankind was given to ability to procreate and the angels were not. This was a revelation from the *Thoughtland*.

I know it shocked me too when I first received this re-knowing, but I can assure you that once you can see it, you cannot deny, that there is more to the story than what you have been told.

When historian continued to mesh together timeframes and events into a narrative that suited a particular purpose, it created something very different than the truth. Everything became woven into a fabric that covered everything but kept nothing warm, for the truth was not in it.

Many names have been given to describe the Holy Spirit, Holy Shekinah, the Dove, and The Comforter among others. The promise of the Holy Shekinah or Holy Spirit is that when a human life chooses to walk with the Holy Spirit, they will never walk alone and will have a continuous tie to the Most High above.

The Most High God because of the connection through you (the Children of the Light) has a foothold on the earth and works through, (you) and those connections of thoughts, words, and deeds. It was the Holy Spirit who sealed the Children of the Light in the epic battle in the heavens between the children of The Most High and a faction seeking to overthrow the very throne of their Creator.

This connection to you, allows the Most High to have hope that all earthly humans can one day so to speak, "see the Light", and return to the true source and forsake the darkness of their existence.

If the overthrow was successful I would be telling a very different story but the battle for the throne was not successful and the Savior of the day was recognized for the very first time.
The Savior symbol and The Christ symbol became synonymous that day after the epic battle that is forever recorded in Gnostic history.

The warriors are recognized as Archangel Michael and Archangel Gabriel. Archangel Gabriel lost and was expelled from the heavens to the lower realms which included the earth and thus was the beginning of the end the glorious days of the first earth age.

It is said, that a third of the angels chose to leave with Archangel Gabriel for life in the lower realms, but the rest who chose to fight with Archangel Michael remained in the upper heavens.

However, it wasn't just being expelled, it was the loss of the privileges afforded those that lived in the Earthly Garden of Eden, the magnitude of the loss of privileges that were no longer available to them, did not sink in, I suspect, until the lockout of Heaven was secured.

The passage that talked about the pain of childbirth, and having to work to survive only applied to those being expelled from the higher heavens. So from that moment on, they became disconnected from the Light and had to rely on their own resources and abilities for the first time in their life, in ways they had no understanding or knowledge thereof.

The Christ that we are familiar with was established firmly in the heavens as our Savior, the defender of the faithful, the savior in battle; the right hand of The Most High. This was not an earthly occurrence but was later retold and retold until it became a well- known story of early salvation. It also became the symbol of the iconic image of the Mother and Son, instead of the Mother and her Children of the Light.

The first earth age was a matriarchal society where the bloodline came directly from the mother and the inheritance came from the mother. The gift of the Holy Spirit was passed from the mother. Everything was as above so below.

During the first earth age there was no division between the heavens and the earth that prevented travel between the two worlds. The wonders of the earth were built, all of the needs mentioned in Genesis chapter one was created and the earth was truly a Garden of Eden.

This was truly a beautiful and complete paradise for the creation of the first humankind to inhabit. We will never know how long this paradise lasted, but it was a very long time and many things that are recorded in the bible actually happened during the first earth age when

God and the angels did indeed intermingle with the first humankind that lived on the earth.

It was written, that the tone of the writing dug up from ancient manuscripts was so very different that historians could not place the attributes of them to any of the known scribes of biblical times. Their language and tone were just too different from the language and the tone of what was used in the language of the second earth age. It went from loving and happiness; reverence and joy; to anger and vengeance; envy and hate. It is no wonder that the first earth age did indeed have to come to an end.

But my search is for the Creator who would be the God of the Children of the Light. My search is for the place that I can pinpoint to, as the single best place to put my stake in the ground and say this is it. That is why those two phrases were always so important, for they are foundational to our basic understanding.

Creation of life on earth takes a man and a woman, which is an earthly construct that did not require the Most High's participation, for it is stated in the bible that the LORD breathed into his nostrils the breath of life. Genesis 2:7. It is important to note here what breathing in life, as it relates to, "in our image according to our likeness" really means.

On the highest levels of creation the essence of oneself is taken out and put into another being in order to replicate itself. In the working theory of as above so below, this was also done by the LORD of the Earth realm. By breathing into the man formed from the dust of the earth, the man received the essence of his LORD, which also included the sinful nature of the seven deathly sins and hence forward there was sin in the nature of earthly man. Thus began new life on earth.

But to understand why the phrase "as above so below" is not exactly the same we must look at how the thought of eternal life effected a change in the first earth age inhabitants that led to the sealing of it, and the creation of the second earth age.

The parameters to enter the gates of heaven from that time on required that one had to be so pure as to fit through the eye of the needle, meaning they had no baggage, no sin, where washed clean, by the purification process, whatever that may be, for only heaven knows for sure.

The loving nature of the feminine energy when all was spirit and moved through the heavens and upon the earth with ease in love and light was a creative energy having the divine ability to create at will whatever the heart desired.

It was a glorious time, unimaginable in the world we live in today. This was one of the many meanings of the phrase "as above, so below." It truly did exist in the first earth realm. It was Utopia, a paradise, full of the true Songs of Solomon, complete with an eternal life of love, joy and happiness. But when the seven deadly sins entered into the realm, discord and disharmony were sown, and the very foundations of the heavens were shaken, the gateway to the heavens had to be closed after the cleansing through an ethereal flooding. As above so below no longer existed, for those who chose the path of the "fallen". Their access to the feminine energy source that provided everlasting life was lost and their sojourn in the wilderness began. And thus, you have the story of the Exodus.

It is not pretty and I take no pride in uncovering the truths of the bible. But, if we are to save ourselves in the midst of battle, we have to be properly armed with all the knowledge and understanding, we can possibly acquire, that lead us to the wise choices, we will be forced to make. All of humankind will depend on it. For it is not the hope that the formed shall be forsaken and forever lost, but that they will free themselves and seek the Light.

In Genesis chapter two, the first four verses belong to chapter one, for they are really just a continuation of the Garden of Eden in its seventh day, which probably lasted thousands, if not millions of years.

Then in verse five of chapter two we get a glimpse of what life after expulsion was really like. There were no plants and no herb in the fields and no one to till the ground... This passage can allude you for the Garden of Eden on Earth was a lush with life and with everything human life needed in chapter one. In chapter two there was nothing and no one to till the ground and no water- which we know is referring to Divine Living Water (God). So now we have the introduction of the first formed beings of the second earth age, who were not the created beings of the first earth age? Is it possible that the two earth ages exist side by side in some alternate reality? Did the first Earth Age actually pass away or does it still exist, and is just not accessible to those who believe in the Most High?

The Adam and Eve story was a distortion of the facts and a story retold in the second earth age as if it was in the beginning. Their story was told in Genesis chapter two.

It is in chapter two of Genesis that the new second earthly ruler is introduced as LORD.

It is in Chapter two that the LORD formed man from the dust (earth) and breathed into his nostrils the breath of life and the man became a living being. The earthly formation of man was an incomplete being for something was missing, something was broken. This formed being did not have the ability to reproduce and so the earth remained barren, which could also be a metaphor for without population. Therefore, a mate for the first earthly Adam was formed from a part of him to be his mate.

It always confused me as to why in one chapter you refer to God and in the next it is Lord, I am so glad that this question is finally answered and I am no longer confused. Do not be deceived, as children of the Most High! You answer to no Lord for your spiritual salvation. "Render unto Caesar what is Caesar's and unto God what is God's", meaning Caesar (LORD) may have your worldly possessions, but only the Most High can have your soul.

The ability to create at will is shown in the many temples, pyramids, statures and things of amazing skill was put on the earth thousands of years before the Stone Age was recorded to leave reminders of the glory of the past, which still cannot be explained today.

Right in Front of Us

The "Thoughtland" was busy talking to me last night and this is the answer to this question on the feminine, I received last night. You know how something is staring you right in the face and you cannot see it no matter how long you look at it? Well that is what conditioning will do to you. It is correct to say Mother and child, it is not correct to say Mother and son. She is our Mother and we are her children. The iconic symbol is the reminder, but we have been deceived into believing it meant something else to fit into the new storyline of earth.

There are always cracks in the veil, tares in the fabric, and holes in the timeline that give light on a phrase which harkens from a distant past history. These are the amazing crumbs that help shed light on a needed piece of information that has great relevance to our re-knowing.

The statement by The Christ of the Age of "Behold your Mother" is probably the most profound statement in the bible for the learning of "from wince cometh our help". It was stated that our help cometh from the Lord.

I have to stop right here again because the word "Lord" can be very deceptive and mean almost anyone who sets themselves up as a Lord. We, who are the Children of the Light, should never be deceived or mislead into using titles not ordained and attributed to the hierarchy of The Most High.

There is a saying, "to be wise as a serpent", and when reading the bible one must be, lest you be profoundly deceived.

The biblical scholars has put so many names out there that are supposed to belong to the Original that you have to wonder, who are they trying to confuse and infuse?

The Alpha and the Omega is all inclusive and the need for other names to explain the "ALL" is totally unnecessary, unless something nefarious is underfoot.

Back to "Behold you Mother", when Christ made this statement he was talking to the Children of the Light that resided on the earth through the will of the Most High to do the work of God, who had lost sight of who they originally were. And to the fallen angels, and children of the darkness, so that they too might have salvation, through the introduction and reintroduction of the Holy Spirit, and asking them to take the Holy Spirit into their fleshly home, thus giving every being a chance of salvation and a way home.

The passage speaks volumes about how the meanings of spiritual knowing were altered and when you put them into a physical and earthly setting, how everything takes on entirely different meanings.

Definition: Feminine

At some point in the fourteen hundreds, there was an effort to define "feminine" for the dictionary. It was very telling what they came up with.

- Pertaining to a woman or girl
- Having qualities traditionally ascribed to women as sensitivity or gentleness
- Belonging to the female sex; female

And then there was a special note:

Noting or pertaining to, one of the three genders of Latin, Greek, German or one of the two genders of French, Spanish or Hebrew. Effeminate (Latin, Greek, German) vs. felare to suck, suckle, she who suckles; state of being feminine

It seems that the Italians, Greeks and Germans had identified a third human species which they called effeminate.

This is a significant finding that has escaped my knowledge bank until now. Clearly there were two distinct groups of humans on the planet at that time, which were different enough to be classified differently by different groups. It seems we are still in denial, and still trying to make everyone fit into a two-seater when we need a three-seater.

It is also telling that the split before the two are essentially old world and new world.

But wouldn't the world have just been better if the said identification didn't lead to the trying to eradicate an entire species of humans?

I think it is very interesting to know that the Latin, Greek and German dictionaries all recognized a third gender designation while the French, Spanish or Hebrew only recognized two.

Clearly there was a difference between the two groups that caused this big difference and it bears further looking into. But for right now, have eyes to see.

An amazing occurrence happened in the bible that the ordinary church person is seemingly unaware of, which is when the bible begins. There seems to be two energies working in tandem in the creation of the two worlds comprising the "As above, so below" universes.

These two energies moved with thought commands and motion which was sometimes force. It was right there from the beginning of Genesis that the Great Feminine Energy of creation was erased from the bible. It was there that the greatest deception in the history of the world started. It happened in the very beginning of the re-write of history.

When you take the Mother Energy of all creation out of history and replace it with male energy it of course changes the very nature of history from one of nurture to one of force and might. It was all we were left with, and we are still operating under the illusion of the rightness of force and might today.

Definition: Holy Spirit

The Spirit in the Hebrew is feminine, the Shekinah. Therefore the Holy Spirit is feminine. In John 6:63 it states that, "*it is the spirit that gives life, the flesh is useless.*"

According to the Gospel of Saint Thomas the Holy Spirit is so vitally essential the true Christian way, do not be deceived.
Jesus said, "*He who seeks will find, and he who knocks will be let in. Knock on the door of the Holy Sanctuary; seek invitation by the Holy Spirit…*"

The pathway is to assist you through your upward spiral; the pathway is made available to you; the pathway is through the Holy Spirit.

Holy Spirit; the Divine Mother; the Most High God

The attributes speak volumes to the truth. It says that not everyone was fooled into thinking that the Most High was a masculine energy.

The Glory of the Most High is revealed in the colors chosen for symbolism and is the key in all written and oral history.

These divine attributes of the Feminine is represented by these titles:

- The Holy Mother
- The Holy Spirit
- Mother Mary
- Mother of the Church
- Virgin of Light
- The Woman of Zion
- *The Woman of Heavenly Jerusalem*
- The Cosmic Woman
- *Mary as Our hope of Salvation*
- Mary is Queen of the Universe
- *Woman crowned with Stars*
- Queen of Angels
- Joy of Israel
- *Ark of the Covenant*
- *Morning Star*

These are all wonderful titles that are attributes to the Holy Spirit and the Holy Mother by the Catholic Religion and by definition the Hebrew religion as well. Yet we are left with no hint of the Feminine in the church today. While there is no problem with describing the Mother of All, no one ever describes the titles of the Father. Yet somehow we are led to believe that Jesus the Christ somehow created himself and his mother and then made her the mother of the church, while he is God the Father, God the Son and God the Holy Spirit, confused yet? I think so, because she has been knocked off her throne and out of heaven.

The Holy Spirit is the Mother God of humankind.

The Most High God is the creator of all the Universes and until we get this hierarchy right we will never pray correctly to the power source we are seeking for our salvation.

In order to accurately describe the Most High God in a way that will foster a greater understanding of the name, I will rely on the recorded terms throughout history.

One of the oldest known to us is the *Virgin of Light* which creates and recreates itself.

The Egyptians referred to this as the *Body of Nut* – the woman of the heavens. Her body hovered over as the sky over the earth below shielding it and gives birth to the sun each day. Which means we owe our existence on a daily basis to the Holy Spirit for without "Her" birthing the sun on a daily basis, where would we be?

The Woman of the Stars, manifesting our reality as the Woman of Zion and the Woman of Heavenly Jerusalem, which is the three-fold Feminine Power that we have never recognized.

This was the truth of old, which we no longer hear, read, or are told of this profound truth.

Definition of Blue White Light

The symbolism of Blue White Light is the color symbol of the Mother herself nothing missing, nothing broken; the Alpha and the Omega; all inclusive, having the complete ability to create at will.

The colors have been wrongly attributed to the Star of David of the earthly period, but since these colors really belong to the Feminine which is of the highest order and magnitude and represents the Holy Spirit Mother.

In order to correctly attribute the iconic colors of blue and white to their rightful place, let's look at why the *Thoughtland* pointed them out to me.

Blue is the color of the sky and the sea it symbolizes:
- Trust
- Loyalty
- Wisdom
- Confidence
- Intelligence
- Faith
- Truth
- Heaven
- White symbolizes:
- Light
- Goodness
- Innocence
- Purity
- Virginity
- Perfection
- Safety
- Cleanliness
- Successful beginning
- Wholeness
- Sincerity
- Protection

- Faith
- Humility
- softness
- Equal balance of all the colors spectrum both positive and negative

Phraseology: Behold the Mother

The passages speak volumes about the misinterpretation and intentional changing of the passage meaning. When you change a spiritual meaning to a physical meaning, the whole interpretation has to change to accommodate the lie, which is what happened when trying to take an ageless work and modernize it into a two thousand year old setting. The ageless originals spoke of things as they were, not as man's comprehension would have them be.

In John 19:27, as Yeshua introduced the Holy Spirit, his mother, to his disciple and told him to welcome the Holy Spirit into his body (home) the indwelling of the Holy Spirit happened here. It was the model for the salvation of the earth's humankind.

"Behold your Mother", said Yeshua (the Son of God). Profound statement, when you stop to think that this is not about a physical person at all. The modern bible wanted to reduce the significance of the Mother by making her a physical human, while God remained a Spiritual Being, never in the physical, until they later decided that The Son would be the Father as well, and take a physical role and a spiritual role.

This never made any sense to me until now. There is no likeness in the spiritual realm and in the physical realm. We are taught to think there is, but the truth is, there isn't. We have been duped. We have been fooled into believing that we were serving an awesome God, a patriarchal family that has our best interest and salvation at heart. We are told it is God will, that we be subservient to man because it is God's will. That God's son died for our sins and we owe everything to him.

But Yeshua said, "Behold your mother", he did not say behold your father, he did not say take your father in, he said take your mother in.

The talmid accepted the Mother of the Christ as his spiritual God (Mother).

The Re-Knowing is upon us, all of us, for the corruption of the world is at an all-time high, and it is ripe for a correction. If the correction is coming, it will not be a time to be blind to the fact. For if you are, you will be easily, yet once again, led down the wrong path.

There are principalities of the earth which will be doing battle with the spiritual forces of the heavenly realms, and only those who can discern the truth will know which is which and whose side they want to be on.

It will not be a time to be wishy washy; no fence sitters allowed; no one will be allowed to sit this one out. You will be affected one way or another. I prefer to choose my destiny and not leave it up to chance.

Another thing that this has told us is the disciples knew of their spiritual mother for Yeshua told his beloved talmid, which means pupil, student of the Torah, a Torah scholar, or one well versed in the Hebrew Law. Therefore, it seems to me that the corruption must have come after the first five books were written.

In order to break free from the mundane and advance our soul on its journey back to the Eternal Source, we cannot stay in darkness and unknowingness.

In a world where we simply languish in ways that are designed to keep our minds off of our divine destiny and rooted in the diseased world of selfishness; where what we accumulate, watch, do, and think is destined to sink us deeper into the abyss, which is designed to make our ascension ever more distant and remote. We must know what to seek.
In order to react to the Light, we must first be conscious that the Light does exist. However, increasingly, we are led to believe that the Light is only for the leaders and we are just the flock they lead. But know this; it is not actually true, for in the statement by Yeshua of *Behold your Mother* the powerful presence of the Mother, the introduction of the *Holy Spirit, Mother-God*. This statement does not get to the prominence in our biblical culture that it deserves, for if it had, it would have changed the course of history and nothing would be as it is now.

The coming of the Christ was to provide a wayshower of the path back to the Eternal Source and historians rewrote and therefore derailed his mission either through ignorance or on purpose. Either way we were left the worse for wear because of it.

Energy is a word we are not taught to respect outside of its utility as a resource. But energy is a vital inner connective entity, one that must be nurtured and nourished daily as a life-force with the cosmic world and the Cosmic Mother.

While the mundane aspects of earthly energy sources can have other positive or negative effects on the earth, ethereal energy can also have both negative and positive effects on our spiritual and physical well being here on earth.

There were safe guards and practices available to us to grow, nourish and protect our energy fields from the harmful daily bombardment of negativity coming through the airwaves, people and military programs designed to keep us in the dark. But were we ever told about these safeguards?

The Ancient Eastern View of the Divine Mother

The tenants of all there is, to what we believe, did not originate in the West, but was brought here from wherever humans first originated on the earth plane. We are very modern and very literal in our thinking of the, who, what and how of our creator.

One of the greatest teachings of my mentor and teacher taught was that truth is truth, and if you find truth in one religion it will show up in another, for it does not change, people do. So now, whenever I having a knowing, a new truth, I seek confirmation of this in other truths. It is a very validating and enlightening experience to receive not only truth from the universe, but to also receive confirmation from that same universe.

We are here not to invent the truth, but to rediscover it for ourselves and to pass it on to others. If I find out some truth and do not pass it on, I am not fulfilling my responsibilities of being a good steward of the truth placed in me. The act of offering proof that my newly found truth existed long before me is a way of confirmation that it indeed needs to be told and retold to the unsuspecting children of God.

One amazing thing I did not know is such a small thing that need great light shed on it is this:
There is a connection between the Eastern "Aum" and the Holy Spirit (Divine Mother).
But further:

- Hindus – Aum
- Modammedan – Amin
- Christian – Amen
- And the knowledge that in the beginning was the Word!

I myself have for a long time taken it upon myself to say amen, amen and amen to end an important prayer, I didn't know why I started it, but continued because it just felt right. But obviously I wanted in some very profound way to acknowledge my Creator.

The truths of the Ancient Eastern avatars, sages and saints, I will list here so that we all can see that East did meet West before it was taken out of the bible and lost in our dialogue in the churches and temples of worship.

Their enlightenment:
"The formless Absolute is my Father, and God with form is my Mother." –Kabir
"Nameless indeed is the source of creation. But things have a mother and she has a name." – Lao Tzu

---

"The macrocosm and microcosm rest in the Mother's womb. Now do you see how vast She is?" – Sri Ramakrishna
"Reality has two-levels, one of which may be called the absolute, acosmic, or transcendental level and the other the relative, cosmic, or phenomenal." – Swami Nikhilananda

These have become the defined by the definition we use today to describe all beings *above and below as male and female.*

"At the phenomenal level one perceives the universe of diversity and is aware of one own individuality or ego, whereas at the transcendental level, differences merge into an inexplicable non-dual consciousness. Both these level s of experience are real from their respective standpoints, though what is perceived at one level may be negated at the other." – Swami Nikhilananda
"She is Procreatrix, Nature, the Destroyer, and the Creator." – Swami Nikhilananda
"Thou art the creator; thou art the destroyer by thy prowess; and thou art the protector." – the Upanishads
"Maya makes all things: what moves, what is unmoving. On son of Kunti, that is why the world spins, turning its wheels through destruction."- Sri Krishna
"The mother was in sole charge of 'management of the bodily and spiritual worlds.'" –Avatar Zarathustra
"Wisdom: 'operates everything.'" – Solomon
"...she is the Mother of the Universe, identical with the Brahman of Vedanta, and with the Atman of Yoga. As eternal lawgiver...She is the Supreme Mistress of the cosmic play, and all objects, animate and inanimate, dance by Her will. Even those who realize the Absolute in niroikalpa Samadhi are under Her jurisdiction as long as they live on the relative plane. – Swami Nikhilananda
"Wisdom penetrates and permeates everything that is, every material thing." – Solomon
"After the creation the Primal Power (the Mother) dwells in the universe itself. She brings forth this phenomenal world and then pervades it." – Sri Ramakrishna
"The Divine Mother revealed to me that it is She Herself who has become man." – Avatar of Dakshineswar
"Wisdom hath built her house; she hath hewn her seven pillars." – Avatar of Dakshineswar

The teachings, my mentor and teacher taught, about the seven chakras of the body, and their relationship to the universe, which for me makes the health of the body's chakra system paramount to our ability to connect to the universal Mother. So for me the seven pillars and the seven chakras are one and the same. Our body is her house that She has made ready to dwell in.

"Every human being is essentially a soul (the Child of God or Atman, one with the Father), covered with a veil of Maya (the Mother)." - Sri Krishna

Here the ancient Eastern sages, brings our attention, to the Iconic Mother and Child of the Western religions. However, they see the children as immortals, which in the west only salvation can save the mortal soul. No mention of immortally for the children of God?

Is this the break between the east and the west or it is just two different very true knowing, but we as a society have tried unsuccessfully to make one truth?

If my premise of Genesis 1 and 2 are indeed correct then there is great daylight between the western and eastern thoughts and belief systems

But let us continue to look at it from the Eastern immortal child of God standpoint. What does an immortal child do?

"That the purpose of life is enlightenment. The purpose of life is that the undying soul should travel out from God, into the world, where, after eons of spiritual evolution and enlightenment, it will learn that it and God are one. The purpose of life, viewed from the Creator's standpoint, is that God should meet God, and through that meeting, enjoy His own bliss. The Father created the Mother, who went on to create trillions of forms – prodigal children, embodied souls – which left the Father and traveled in the realm of matter, until every form comes to know itself as God."

In the west we have the Trinity. We speak of the speak of the parables and we speak of the end of the journey of Christ, what we don't speak of it the true meaning of any of these things as it relates to our true self and nature. But in here lies the secret of the cracking of the mustard seed. The seed is hard and it is indeed very small but it has the ability to grow into a fully matured tree, such as the Tree of Life of the ancient Hebrew faith, which is much like the seven chakra activations which also take a long time to achieve maturity.

"These waves (arise) from the Great Ocean and merge again into the Great Ocean. From the Absolute to the relative, and from the Relative to the Absolute." – Sri Ramakrishna

"It has been revealed to me that there exists an Ocean of "Consciousness" without limit (i.e. the Father). From it come all things of the relative plane (i.e. the Mother), and in it they merge again." – Sri Ramakrishna

This merging is the ALL, nothing missing nothing broken, the Alpha and the Omega. So much like what I received from the

"Thoughtland", so ancient a knowing, so designed to make sense of everything we have no way of knowing, perceiving or making sense out of ourselves, and something that no clergy has related to us for either they have not been taught this knowing, or they did not understand it or believe it. Either way I did not receive it in any traditional church. There are many representations of the inactive God and the active God given to us in the bible, in the Eastern religions and in the Egyptian hieroglyphs.

The Bible States:

In the beginning God created the heaven and the earth.
And the earth was without form, and void; and darkness was upon the face of the deep. And the Spirit of God moved upon the face of the waters. - KJV

The Eastern Hindi religion Shakti is the divine female principle of force, the energy provider behind everything for without energy there is no power. Shiva on the other hand is said to be as limitless as the sky; as unchanging as it is formless and unknowable. But of course that is at its' highest form. But even they recognize that the real power lies in the use of energy in motion. Thus, the role of the divine force is secure.

Egyptian myth has the sky god Osiris killed by his brother Seth cut up into 14 different pieces and hidden all over the planet. Isis uses her magical powers to locate 13 of the pieces to put Osiris back together. Horus grew up to avenge his father by waging war with Seth for the throne. Horus is the representative Christ Horus the hawk-god. It further states that Osiris descends into the underworld, where he became the lord of that domain.

The interesting thing about this which ties into the narrative of all the major religions is that it is Osiris who is rendered dormant and Isis who moves to and fro using her magical and restorative powers to return Osiris to his final resting place and spiritual domain.

The Western religions prefer to have a dominant male presence that over time has managed to completely change the position of the divine mother from a subservient role in creation, to no role in religion or in life in general. But just because the facts have been altered doesn't make the truth go away or be less valid. It must be very important if so many were willing to obfuscate the mere mention of *the divine mothers'* role in our creation and salvation.

By establishing that this is not new thought, is very important, because it is the re-knowing that will help guide us to fulfill our true potential; by cracking open the mustard seed, and letting the Tree of Life located in the core of our being flourish and thrive.

Our Mother of Creation wants nothing less!

Aspirations revisited
The measure of human growth has been defined for us
as the material attainment of stuff, the more we accumulate,
the more we have grown.
But material goals tie us deeper to the earth,
and only give us a false sense of eternal attainment.
For this is not our forever home,
however, our real home will continue to get more distant
as our aspirations are steered to the material,
and away from the Holy Spirit of the Most High God.

Chapter Ten

Looking Back and Reflecting

We are a microcosm of the macrocosmic universe.
By traveling the world it has a way of opening up oneself to the realities that there is more out there.

When I went to Egypt in nineteen ninety nine, I was completely awestruck by the majestic nature of the remnants of the ancient world as it was juxtaposed against the modern world of today.

Everything was on a larger than life scale. Everything inside of me knew something was out of place and definitely out of order.

As we traveled further up the Nile and into Abu Simbel in Nubian country near the border with Sudan. I was amazed at the many black statures that were immense in size but lay on their backs as if to have been stand up right would have told a different story than the one put forth. Which was very much like the small boy statue of Tutankhamun, not, and at all like the one you see with the golden mask.

This made a deep impression on me, I cannot speak for my fellow travelers but I was in deep physical agony about a past I had known nothing about. I was intuitively informed to pay attention and to look beyond the surface and see a different truth. What I came away with was questions having questions and at that time no answers.

That was nineteen ninety nine, and as with everything else those questions were added to a growing list, I needed to find answers for during my time here on earth.
I had known for a long time that I was not here to be a vegetable, but to learn and to share what I learned. The phrase "knowledge is power" has had a constant presence in my understanding of my journey. The need to know and the need to dissimulate go hand in hand with my reason for being here.
While I love having a good life, I still know I cannot have it at the expense of my mission. The ultimate mission is to shed light on the truth whenever and however I can, using all the God given tools of my blessings.

I was blessed to go to Egypt. I was blessed to see beyond the veil of what is regularly and routinely shown. I was blessed to see and feel the spirit of the ancestors, so that I could later draw from the experience to learn, and be opened up to more ancient history and wisdom to share.

It was years later when I learned just how different my experience was from the rest of the group I traveled with.
We were all on a spiritual quest of sorts. Each knowing in their hearts some of the reasons for this adventure, but I actually didn't know how important this trip was to my future growth, knowledge and understanding of universal underpinnings would be until much later.

It was as if the trip was the gateway, the portal, the opening one has to go through to gain knowledge. A knowledge that is not automatically given, but without this opening, one cannot get to the next level of understanding of what one has been privy to witness. Nor can you receive the seeds of wisdom from the *Thoughtland* designed to further your growth.
In Egypt, I conquered some major fears which to this day, I am reminded, that the mind is stronger than any fear the darkness can impose, and there is no negative tie that binds that cannot be broken.

It was in Egypt that I learned not to believe in false gods; nor to take anything on face value. And to know that almost everything, if not everything, has another meaning that needs to be explored and weighed against the evidence currently and previously presented as fact. From the bible to all forms of history, for, all that is written is not so.

Spiritual journeys always bring enlightenment to your soul, and serve to awaken the spiritual you to the illusion of your present existence. This awakening urges you to awake from the trance state you currently occupy, and become aware of your new eyes and ears.

A few years back I asked a dear friend, who had arranged the Egyptian trip and who was also a part of the church I belonged to, if she could tell me what the black temple we visited was made out of and where it was located. I had exhausted my Google search and could not find it. I intuitively thought it was made out of Obsidian but wanted to be sure. To my surprise, neither she nor our Egyptologist tour guide knew of such a temple, and both stated we had not gone there.

As far as they knew, it did not exist, but of course it did. I was there! I went through the portal and into the silence of the majestic completely black temple. I was asked while I was there what I felt and I remember saying I felt sad. I remember later thinking, I should have said something more profound than just that, still believing that we had made a special trip there just so that I could see it, as I was the only black person in the group. But the truth is what comes into your mind first is truth and what I felt was sadness.

I wish everyone could have seen it; it was so beautiful against the bright blue sky. It was perfect looking, pristine, regal, grander than grand, new un-aged, untouched and never occupied, silent and completely empty. Through it all was the silent sound of sadness.

I didn't know it then, but what I felt was the sadness of the Mother! Of what could have been, but never came to pass.
It has stayed with me as one of the greatest memory of the trip and until I learned that it was only seen and experienced by me, I thought the shared experience was for the enlightenment of all, but it was just for me, that was when real unadulterated awe set in. I remain so still.

Now I bow down to the *Thoughtland* in total amazement that I have been chosen to see beyond my present circumstance and to glean knowledge on a higher level and to be able to obtain a greater understanding of what the faith passage means " *Now faith is the substance of things hoped for, the evidence of things not seen."* Hebrews 11:1 - KJV

There were several other notable experiences on the trip that changed the course of my journey in this lifetime. We were given special permission to enter an underground temple chamber one which was not granted to the general public and one in which you would never even know was available without an Egyptologist who worked for the Museum of Cairo and had considerable knowledge.
My fear of closed places would normally have overcome me and not allowed me to enter such a tight quarter, stepping down narrow steps into the unknown, smelling slightly musty, on any other given day would not have been doable, But, today I was brave as I entered the small chamber where the Egyptian Goddess Nut was holding up the entire sky and giving birth to the sun every morning.
What a wonderful find, so well hidden and so misunderstood by the world. I felt truly blessed especially since the first time I recalled hearing anything about holding up the sky was two years earlier in China. There are Chinese women in leadership meeting they announced proudly that in China they hold up half the sky. If only they knew they once had the power to whole up the entire sky.
I didn't want to leave and was the last one to exist the chamber hearing them calling for me to catch up, finally I climbed out looked around and saw no one, they were all gone, I knew I must hurry, as I rush toward the outside, someone or something compelled me to turn around as I did, there was a priest standing in the middle of the grand hall with the light streaming down on him, as if he came down through the light all dressed in white and as black as could be. In a reflex I snapped the picture, and felt a complete feeling of grace fall upon me. Instantly the scene vanished as if I had not seen it. I scurried to catch up, but remained feeling blessed and connected in a way I had never felt before and for that

matter since. It was a rare spiritual experience. I have had other experiences but none quite like this one. I was forever changed.

The Goddess Nut was my first introduction to the *Divine Mother* concept of ancient times. It remained just a concept, but still left a deep impression that would never go away, and one that kept seeping into my lectures and future writings as I grappled with the knowing, that there was something important there, that I was missing.

A few years later I attended an ecumenical lecture and listened to some faithful Catholic women try to explain their love for Mary, the mother and why they prayed to her daily because the mother was accessible and easy to pray too, but their absolute reverence for Jesus at the same time they felt had to be stated.

At the time I was confused by their seemingly torn allegiances, if they say they love one they must immediately defend the other. It seemed to be a very bi-polar situation, as if intuitively they felt something but felt the need to repress it or explain it away.

As Protestants we just left Mary out all together, we didn't pray to her, consult her, revere her in any way, and all of a sudden I didn't want to just ignore everything anymore, why was Mary left out? How had we become such a male dominated society, that any mention of the mother was a cause for self-recrimination, even if done so with qualifications?

Had religion instead of giving us a clear cut way to experience our faith instead made us schizophrenic over-thinkers, or bi-polar worshipers?

Asking these questions was probably how the deeper dive into Mary began in even though I had made no connections yet, I did had a lot of fragmented thoughts that didn't fit into any scenario I had heard in church I had attended.

If we ever take the bible at its word, it should be when it states *I am Alpha and Omega, the Beginning and the End, the First and the Last.* Revelations 22:13 KJV

Then you would know that God was the sole creator of everything, the originator; the mother; the pregnant one; the birther; the provider; the one who nourishes, the nurturer, the deliverer, which represents the Iconic Mother and Child. It also represents the God of Creation and her Children as seen with the stars above and a halo around their head representing the Light and the moon under their feet representing the earth, which makes her ruler of heaven and earth.

I missed this in Sunday school. I also missed it in Bible Study. I also missed it in my ordination studies. But now armed with new eyes and new ears, it seems that the information is not uniquely mine, it is out here, but of course visible only to the seekers.

I think that the Star of David once may have represented the Divine Mother, those were her colors, until she was relegated to the earthly realm as the earthly mother, then red was added, which changes the whole color vibration in the universe. But notice that they did not get rid of the importance of the blue and white vibration but changed it to a masculine symbol.

The two triangle unification is a symbol of complete integration of the whole nothing missing nothing broken. It is also represents the Bride and the Bridegroom in the wedding chamber. It is one unit, having everything within itself and needing nothing external.

It is a hard concept to grasp but the Divine Mother was and is capable of creation without help and that is why I say now, I know why there was never a father figure. That is also why I say it was never supposed to be the Mother and Son, but the Mother and Child representing the children of God.

Now that light has been shed on our Mother we must look for her children, who are called the Children of the Light and the Children of God.

We are getting closer to the truth of "ALL"...

Identification of the Children

Chapter Eleven

Needle in the Proverbial Haystack

The crumbs of the bible are starting to yield answers.

I hope by now you can see where I am going with my premise, that the truth is right in front of us just waiting for us to see it in the light of day.

Here we are at the intersection of truth and falsehood and the light is ready to take you home to the Iconic Mother and Child.

The true representation of the Mother and her children is seen in the children of light as depicted by the halo around the head in some pictures.

They say, "A picture is worth a thousand words" and it is especially true if you understand the symbolism hidden in it.

- The Mother represents our Creator
- The Child represents the Children of the Mother
- The halo represents the Light
- The Light represents the immortal beings

The Light existed before the foundation of the world as we know it and so did the Children of the Light according to:

Ephesians 1:4-14
"According as he hath <u>chosen</u> us in him <u>before</u> the foundation of the world, that we should be holy and without blame before him in love:
5 Having <u>predestinated</u> us unto the adoption of children by Jesus Christ to himself, according to the good pleasure of his will,
6 To the praise of the glory of his grace, wherein he hath made us accepted in the beloved.
7 In whom we have <u>redemption through his blood</u>, the forgiveness of sins, according to the riches of his grace;
8 Wherein he hath <u>abounded</u> toward us in <u>all wisdom and prudence</u>;
9 Having made known unto us the mystery of his will, according to his good pleasure which he hath purposed in himself:
10 That in the <u>dispensation of the fulness of times</u> he might gather together in one all things in Christ, both which are in <u>heaven</u>, and which are on <u>earth</u>; even in him:

[11] *In whom also we have obtained an inheritance, being predestinated according to the purpose of him who worketh all things after the counsel of his own will:*
[12] *That we should be to the praise of his glory, who first trusted in Christ.*
[13] *In whom ye also trusted, after that ye heard the word of truth, the gospel of your salvation: in whom also after that ye believed, ye were sealed with that holy Spirit of promise,*
[14] *Which is the earnest of our inheritance until the redemption of the purchased possession, unto the praise of his glory."*

This firmly establishes the rightful heirs to the title of the Children of the Light, the Chosen, the Sealed, the inheritors, the Blood Relatives of the Most High God of All.

We cannot argue with something that happened before the beginning of the world, but we can start to reevaluate the assumptions we have held since the beginning for those assumptions have not served us well. The world has indeed become dark and we are further not closer to obtaining the light source of our beginnings.

The crumbs left in the bible tell us to have eyes to see and ears to hear, for there is nothing that can be taken for granted and nothing that can be taken as absolute gospel.

A lot has actually been written about the Children of the Light for us to explore and bring further into the norm.

Phraseology: The Children of the Light?

Jesus said, "If they say to you, 'where did you come from?' say to them, 'we came from the light, the place where the light came into being on its own accord and established [it-self] and became manifest through their image.' If they say to you, 'Is it you?, say 'We are children, we are the elect of the living father.' If they ask you, 'what is the sign of the father in you?' say to them, 'It is movement and repose.'"

From the Gnostic Gospel of St Thomas Page 149 verse 50

The Gospel of St Thomas offered me a treasure trove of information on how to explain the distinction between the children of earth and the children of light.

The symbolism of the blood relationship between the Christ and the Children of Light is important because it represents their shared nature. It cannot be said of all the born children.

For not all can say we came from the place where the light came into existence, or that we carry a sign that indicates movement and repose. This statement does not offer meaning or clarity to most people on the planet, let alone empower them to embrace it without understanding. But it is one of the most powerful understandings a child of light can possess, yet most do not know of it.

The true Children of the Light enjoy privileges they received before the foundation of the world, and before all other being were thought into existence by the Most High God.

Being the first begotten, being Children of Light having the holy essence, the foundational substance running through their veins and having the gift of immortality as a bloodline is as special as it gets and as coveted as it gets.

It also means you are free from the original sin (the contamination of negative thoughts seeded in the DNA) and therefore have no need for salvation from the dominion of earth.

Being a child of light also means being able to move freely and to rest (repose) means you have eternal and everlasting life and that you can ascend and descend between worlds, realms and universes, enjoying new experiences and developing understanding beyond what your life represents in order to be empathic and knowledgeable of the conditions of humankind.

You may see it as a true baptism into the mystical death and resurrection process.

You may also see it as acknowledgement of the indwelling Holy Spirit or as it is called in modern times the "Christ-Spirit", where on your brow you bear the sign of initiation or seal.

The seal is the holy sign of the covenant of the anointed ones of God. It is this sign that empowers you to move freely between worlds, realms and universes. The seal may also be represented in Egyptian history as the divine connection to the "All Seeing Eye"

The Children of Light exist in this world but intuitively know it is not their home, even if they are unaware why they know this. They also know that the dark side is not their way, even if they don't know why. No matter which situation they are placed into them, they will seek a silver lining and try to make the best of any situation.

The saying "never judge a book by its cover" is very appropriate for the Children of Light for they may look and act just like you, but it doesn't mean they are like you. They agenda is different they assignment will always lead them to do something good, even if you cannot see it or feel it, for they operate according to the plan of God not the will of man. The other old saying that is very appropriate is, "You may be entertaining angels unaware." But just a note of precaution here, it could also be a fallen angel.

In their journeys they may have to venture into the lower realms and worlds but ultimately their path will turn homeward, and back to the light from which they came.

Their travels may take many paths and they will take in much knowledge, not apparent on the surface plane, for they also travel through dreams, through mediation, and through the transmigration process upon death, just as the Christ of each Age does.

I believe that all realms, worlds, and universes occupy the same space, and one excellent example of why I believe this to be true, is the stories that are told from people who have experienced a near death experience (NDE). They tell of seeing a light of going through a tunnel and meeting people on the other side. It happened in minutes not hours or days, and while their bodies never leave the bed. So they are actually in the same time and space, occupying a different reality.

Ordinary people do not have eyes to see, or ears to hear these realms, but they exist and are ever so close. They are well travels at night in our dreams and are food for thought for writers and spiritual beings, seeking to know what is not spoken or taught.

As one works in the light they will be guided to do something to further the process of bringing light into the world. There is no such thing as a small deed for every small deed joins with the larger design for world peace and world harmony between those who are of the light and those who could be Children of God.

Now we come to a very sticky observation and not everyone will want to acknowledge this, but I want to make the distinction between Children of the Light and Children of God.

We can all become Children of God, but only the chosen, elected and sealed before the foundation of the earth are the Children of Light. Their existence is used to help bring the awareness that the masses of earth can become Children of God. The way of the Christ is the salvation, the teachings of Christ is to show the redemption path, but sadly the teachings have all but been eliminated through the watered down process of their teaching, and through the constant attention to morality instead of spirituality. When all of our attention is on what our neighbor is doing, it ends of taking our attention away from our own growth and development. When we listen to the interpretation of the word instead of meditating on the word, so we can receive the inter-knowing that is meant for us, we are not open to receiving the true word of God.

"But to all that did receive him to those who have yielded him her allegiance, he gave the right to become children of God, begotten, not by blood, nor by carnal desire, nor by man's willing, but by God." (1:10-13)

The Gospel of St John
There is so much here but just a few things I want to point out to you. The first is the phrase "yielded him her allegiance" the "him" is referring to the Christ and the "her" is referring to the Holy Spirit.

The second thing I want to point is the phrase "begotten, not by blood..." which takes me back to Ephesians and the "chosen" before the foundation of the world. The Chosen were "begotten" before there were men with carnal desires, because men were created on the earth plane. We have been misled into thinking that the "chosen" was an earthly occurrence and that we could trace it back through some linage and know who the chosen are today. But to do so we would have to be able to trace all the way back to God, and to the origin of all there is, and we have not been able to do that yet, not even with all the research for the God Particle are we even close. You can tell though, that for some, there is a serious need to know about unanswered things, which keep nagging at humanity's core.

So just as surely as I believe the Chosen were begotten before the foundation of the world, I am just as sure that there is no earthly way to disprove my convictions of the origins of heavenly beings and earthly beings.

I remind you here again of the wording of:

Ephesians 1:3-6
Blessed be the God and Father of our Lord Jesus Christ, who has blessed us with every spiritual blessing in the heavenly places in Christ,[4] just as He chose us in Him before the foundation of the world, that we should be holy and without blame before Him in love, [5] having predestined us to adoption as sons by Jesus Christ to Himself, according to the good pleasure of His will, [6] to the praise of the glory of His grace, by which He made us accepted in the Beloved.

Also 1 Peter 1:4-5
Through these he has given us his very great and precious promise, so that through them you may participate in the divine nature, having escaped the corruption in the world caused by evil desires.

Clearly you can see that even in the watered down state of the Bible the differences are in plain sight for all to see.
Before the foundation of the world there was darkness in the void and nothing came to light there.

The whole void, darkness and light scenario can also be allegorical if you look at it in a different light.

Void – can be when there is a complete absence of light and darkness is the absence of light, making them interchangeable when used in the text.

Children of the Light do not belong to the night (darkness) this phraseology is used in the English bible.

Your light comes from the Spirit of God.

The nature of God is love and the Children of Light should emulate the nature of God. However although you are normal in every way and have all of the trapping of the world you still are predestined to assist humanity through the many changes coming. Even if you don't know it now and even if you don't know how, when the time comes, you will be summoned, called into the action, you are predestined to fulfill, but have no fear, you are qualified and are able to perform your role; your life experiences has prepared you to do your part. Know that at the appropriate time you will be ready.

Remember, you were predestined, elected and sealed to be of help for the whole of humanity, in a way that is best suited for the gifts that God has given you, and nurtured in your spirit.

In the book Decoded New Testament, I found the following passage:

The Lord said, "Blessed is the one who exists before, he came into being for he who exists was and will be."
In the Gospel of St Thomas it states:

"When the elect are awakened they become united in fellowship regardless of race, creed, sex or color."

In another passage in the Gospel of St Thomas it states:

The Lord went into the dye-shop of Priest Levi, He took seventy-two colors; he threw them into the kettle. He took them all out white and he said, "Thus the son of Man came, a dyer, (Light of God, a white Spirit), not a white man.

At the end of every dispensation (Age) it is my belief that the Priest forever after the Order of Melchizedek will appear to offer salvation to those awake enough to have eyes to see and ears to hear. I also believe it is the Children of the Light who will assist with the great awakening.

I had struggled with how the Priest became the white Christ in modern times until my research helped me to uncover the deeper meaning.

It did however open my eyes to the grave misunderstandings and misinterpretations of the scholars which have led to unbelievable suffering by all people of color in the world. The actions that have taken place by a misplaced sense of superiority of one's skin color, has allowed the spirit of love, compassion, generosity, mercy, and forgiveness, to be replaced by total corruption of one's personal morals and morality.

It has allowed people, in the name of religion, to kill without remorse, steal land, pillage and burn, destroy scared sites and oppress all that remained. Light does not mean white just as dark does not mean black, yet the entire world is under the assumption that it is exactly what it means, which therefore means, that everything we value and hold dear is based on a lie, and the foundation of the power structure of the world is flawed beyond measure.

But the heavenly design of the Children of Light is thankfully not bound by skin color or any other "ism" that society has placed upon us and will operate when the time comes at the sole discretion and will of the Most High God.

The Children of Darkness will however be offered salvation if their burdens are light enough to:

- Pass through the eye of the needle,
- Or pass through the narrow gate,
- Or after weighing their heart find it lighter than a feather.

The wicked shall indeed inherit the earth, but for the righteous it was never and will never be their forever home for theirs is the kingdom of heaven. The kingdom of heaven can be defined as the other realms; the other worlds and the other universes, or as the bible says, "in my Father's house are many mansions" John 14:2 (KJV), so it is safe to say that no Child of the Most High God would ever want to just inherit the earth when many universes were a part of inheritance.

Summary: of the Children of the Light?

The Children of the Light means you were created before the foundation of the world and were never a part of the dominion of the powers of the world. It further means that your life and your existence on the earth plane have a very different path and trajectory than those that were and are of the earth plane. One of the most important things the children of the light carry, is the symbolic mustard seed with contains the knowing of the beginning. And in the re-knowing the mustard seed will be cracked open and all who possess it will recognize their Mother, their Purpose and their Divinity.

Now of course this needs explaining, but just as the bible has provided me with answers before, it has provided me with answers this time as well.

The covenant was with the children of the light that they would pass through the eye of the needle and pass by the guardians at the gates and enter into the kingdom of heaven without hindrance.

Children of the light will journey through worlds not known on the physical plane not experienced by mere mortal beings and obtain knowledge that makes them kinder to the differences we find on the earth plane. They can do this because the world of our experience is not the only world in existence. There are heavens and hells and worlds of admixture that are neither, heaven or hell but have the influence of both upon them. All around us are worlds within worlds, as dimensions of space and time that is only consciously seen, heard or felt by those attuned and predisposed to it. The ordinary person does not have eyes to see other than what is in front of them, so the other dimensions are out of reach and out of bounds to them.

Some new definitions must come to light so I can share more information as it comes into my consciousness and into my understanding as I perceive it now.

Additional terminologies that support and promote an elevated understanding of our connection to the universe

Definition: Supernal (su per nal)

Of or relating to the sky or the heavens: celestial; of exceptional quality or extent.
Coming from the divine; emanating from above. Heavenly of or pertaining to heaven or God

When this word was first discovered in my readings, all I knew was that I had never heard it before. Then when I learned what it meant, I immediately understood why I had not heard it before.

It was outside the normal way of addressing unworldly beings. It was always thought that those should be left to science fiction, mythology and fairytales. But "fairytales can come true and it can happen to you." Be not old and set in your ways, but be young at heart and in mind.

Definition: Ethereal

Ethereal is an adjective of Supernal meaning extremely delicate or refined, exquisite; almost as light as air, impalpable; airy; celestial or spiritual

Definition: Angels

A spiritual being believed to act as an attendant, agent, or messenger of God, conventionally represented in human form with wings and a long robe.

Angels represent a class of spiritual beings; a celestial attendant of God.

But just like any other realm of consciousness there are hierarchies at play and the angel hierarchy is no different. There are said to be many levels and a full range of ranks within the angel kingdom with titles and duties that I guess rival any governmental structure.

There are office titles and names given to us, by who knows who, that describe the levels of hierarchy in the Heavenly realms:

- Seraphim
- Cherubim
- Thrones
- Dominations or Dominions
- Virtues
- Powers
- Principalities or Princedoms
- Archangels
- Angels

A synonym for Angel is Saint which is used in the bible a lot instead of Angel. But as you can see the angels rank at the bottom of the totem pole and archangels fare only one rank higher, which is interesting since we never get to see or know this. We are taught that they are as high up the ladder as it gets, and sitting ever so close to the Most High God, when it doesn't seem to be that close at all. But even with this, it is us who are far removed, for we are not even in the celestial sphere, but in the mortal world of earth.

You would think that with all our tithing and all our praying, and all our Sunday morning pew sitting, we would have advanced just a tad bit further up the ladder, but alas, we have not.

Definition: Mortal

Being mortal means you are subject to death, having a finite life span. It further means you belong to this world, from the ground (Earth) you came and to the ground you will return.

Definition: Immortal

One whose soul lives forever, while having the ability to take on a mortal body is said in Greek mythology to be a god or goddess a supreme being or deity. Temples in Greece and in Africa were built to honor the immortals. It refers to one who is not mortal, and is not subject to death or dying and is not able to perish or decay; one who in possession of no earthly substance.

Definition: Incarnation

One who comes into the world for a particular reason or as a particular person, is said to incarnate, such is said of the Christ or other deities'. This occurrence can only happen to the immortals.

Definition: Reincarnation

One who has an immortal soul that can be reborn into another body time after time, until heaven and earth shall pass away, also called the transmigration of the soul, or the state of being reborn.

Definition: Demiurge

Demiurge is the term for the underworld, the netherworld, or the world of flesh which is just another way of describing the material world rather than being in a spiritual body in a spiritual realm. This does two things:
1. It establishes the fact that before the foundation of the world, there was a spiritual realm
2. There were spiritual beings in the spiritual realm.

The Gnostics had knowledge of the two worlds and sought to teach humanity in the ways of spiritual enlightenment, but started to be overshadowed by the dogma of the early churches of the fourth century. The term later became synonymous with a particular hell for most lay people. Which included hell fire and brimstone, not much unlike what exist on the earth plane today, who knew? In all actuality earth can be a place of great light or great darkness depending upon what you carry in your heart. The ancient Egyptians are said to have weighed the heart of the departed on one scale and a feather on the other, and if the heart was as light as a feather the departed were worthy of entering into the gates of heaven, the great after life, or into another realm of existence.

The mythological Adam and Eve were sent to the Demiurge after they lost their spiritual garments and were doomed to labor. Another way of saying they were sent to a "hell" of their own making.

There are even two's here to consider of God versus little "g" of Judah and Israel.

Yahweh is one of the six sons of Yaldabaoth the Demiurge, and was worshipped by Judah Jews, while the Israelites worshipped a different god, the Aryan Nordic Alien "Fallen Watchers" known as the Elohim.

If you can't reconcile this with everything you have been taught, you are not alone. I can't, either, but I have uncovered the knowledge, that there is more than one interpretation of God out there, and you have a right and need to know about them for your own research for your truth.

Definition: Gnostic

Members of early sects of Christians, having knowledge, wrote a collection of ancient religions which embraced the spiritual world and an oneness with God shunning all things in the material world.

Definition: Supernatural

It is the act of existing beyond nature, above the physical world.

These definitions are important in establishing knowledge of things that are unseen but known to many. Things that are called by different names, and placed in mythology and science fiction categories, is no longer serving the greater population, which needs to wake-up. Until we engage in enlightened conversations, that make its' way into the mainstream understanding,   our full understanding of the famous biblical verse, "We walk by faith, not by sight." 2nd Corinthians 5:7(KJV) is incomplete and lacking in substance. If, all that can save us is what we can see and feel, we are doomed, because everything that was built in the glory of Eden has been decimated by the acts of human beings, since the beginning of their sojourn here.

Another important finding is that while here on this earth the children of light though more enlightened than most still are subjected throughout their lifetime here to all of the negativity that exist and are bombarded with the same onslaught of energy that has manifested itself into the earth's atmosphere. It makes it all the more necessary to remind them to "Behold your Mother" and bring them back to center, and to the core of their being; for not one child entered without a purpose, but accomplishing it is simply no easy task, in the present climate of today's world.

Are there angels in the world, in all actuality what I do know is that there are different spirit beings, I call them angels because that is what I was taught so in some way I am continuing to carry out the myth, but with a twist. This I will tell you no matter what you call them, it is just a made up word that we have accepted without ever asking whether or not it was true.

The real question we can ask is, "*Are celestial beings, just another name for beings from another planet?*" Temple walls in Egypt suggest that they are, but either way without knowing what is true we must question what is written and what is told. At its core it is at least a way of saying that they were other worldly, not from this planet.

There are theories floating around the internet, that they are alien beings, but just like taking the Divine Mother out of the Bible, everything should be subjected to in-depth discussions before formulating any concrete decisions on something as important as our faith.

The time for the great awakening or the great sleep is nearing. I choose to be awake, which means I will not willingly let anyone put me to sleep or to let myself continue to live in a trance state.

Before there was this universe
heavenly realms existed,
where the Children of Light,
were created from the infinite immortal source,
and became the Royal bloodline
created at its zero point
resided there
and so it was.

This is the identification of the Children (not angels) of Light!

Into the Unknown

It was dark over the horizon
I forged ahead
Without a light
Determined to see
What lay beyond my sight
Cloaked in fog
With secrets to reveal
A vague iridescent dot
Trailed off in the distance
Directing my steps
So many colors and facets
Played on the landscape that night
Beckoning me forward
With no inkling of what
Might come to be
I was determined
To peek beyond
What I could view
For seeing isn't always
Believing
Just as believing
Isn't always seeing
Arriving
I saw nothing there
Just a jagged cliff
With one false step
Off it I would go
I hesitated
No longer sure
What had brought me
To this point
Why did I come here?
There is seemingly no there, here
Still it is of no consequence
No more hesitation
No more questions
The head disconnected
The body felt nothing
The heart now in silent agreement
That there is

No turning back
So this night
Off the jagged cliff
I plunged
Safely into the Light!

Chapter Twelve

The Bible said of the Children

1 Thessalonians 5:5 (KJV)
"Ye are all children of light and the children of the day we are not of the night, nor of darkness."

This proves that in biblical times there was knowledge of the Children of the Light and the Children of the Darkness. There was an understanding and a knowing of those who came from the Divine Light and those who were formed of the ground as in Genesis Chapter Two. These were knowings only a few privileged people on the planet knew, but the vast world's population only heard such things through mythology, science fiction and good theater with popcorn.

The true inheritors of eternal life or everlasting life, was well established in the bible, but put in the wrong context, in the current historical setting, and not in a universal context of unlimited time, and space or of a time before the beginning of time and space, it held no currency then or now.

Before there was any earth to walk on or any animals to have dominion over, the children of the light were begotten and known through their bloodline.

They would be forever known by their zero point, and their entrance as the primal substance of the original genetic code. Of which Hematologist could have derived at by, the absence of anything foreign, or anything found in the earth's realm.

The Pinpoint

Definition: Zero point

- *Ratio Level of Measurement: "Ratio data has all the features of interval data with the added benefit of true 0 point. The term "true zero point" means that a 0 data value indicates the absence of the object being measured."*

- *Ratio scale – true zero point as the origin*
- *The point or place where something begins, arises, or is derived.*

Something that wasn't there is called the true zero point because what you are searching for you cannot find. There is absolutely no trace of it. But when it moves away from true zero point, it pin points the point of origin.

There have been conversations and written documents on this subject in sacred writings, I will present a few.

"At the center of a circle or a sphere is always an infinitesimal point. The point needs no dimension, yet embraces all dimensions. Transcendence of the illusions of time and space result in the point of here and now, our most primal light of consciousness..." (From Sacred Geometry)

Here I am making the case for the attributes of the Christ as having the same as the "center" and for the Iconic Christ symbolism of the Children of Light, sharing the same essence.

Just as tree rings and the deep layers of glaciers tell scientist things about when and what occurred, so does the absence or presence of live organisms or the substance found in living matter reveal answers to the questions we all want to know such as:

Where did we come from, and when did we come?

Indivisible Point

Indivisible Point is a terminology is from the Hindu, but it seems that all major religious thought, understood that there was definitely a point of entry of existence that was beyond our comprehension.

There are passages found in an even older ancient manuscript known today as the Egyptian Book of the Dead. This name likely bears no relationship to the manuscripts original religious purpose.

Papyrus Ani Book of the Dead is much older than the Naassene Sermon. This

The Naassene Psalm

THIS IS A MODERN BUT SOMEWHAT INELEGANT TRANSLATION OF HIPPOLYTUS:

"The Law of Universal Genesis was the first born NOUS; the second, Chaos shed by the firstborn. The third was received by the soul [.....]

Clad in the shape of a hind She [SOPHIA] is worn away with death's slavery. Now She has mastery and glimpses light: now She is plunged in misery and weeps.

Now She is mourned, and her self rejoices. Now she weeps and is finally condemned.

Now She is condemned and finally dies.

And now She reaches the point where hemmed in by evil, She knows no way out. Misled, She has entered a labyrinth.

Then Jesus said, "Behold, Father, she wanders the earth pursued by evil. Far from thy Breath she is going astray. She is trying to flee bitter Chaos, and does not know how she is to escape. Send me forth, O Father, therefore, and I, bearing the seal shall descend and wander all Aeons through, all mysteries reveal. I shall manifest the forms of the gods and teach them the secrets of the holy way which I call Gnosis [.....]"

THIS IS THE NINETEENTH-CENTURY TRANSLATION AS PROVIDED IN THE *Ante-Nicene Fathers* EDITION OF *Hippolytus, Refutation of All Heresies (Book 5 Chapter 5):*

Here is an earlier version I present so you can see just how the scholars have evolved in their thinking and in their representation of historical writings to you over time. It simply is in stark contrast to what the original writings had left for us as our history.

<u>A much earlier version of the Naassene Psalm sheds light on a dark subject.</u>

"The world's producing law was Primal Mind,
And next was First-born's outpoured Chaos; And third, the soul received its law of toil:
Encircl'd, therefore, with an acqueous form, With care o'erpowered it succumbs to death.
Now holding sway, it eyes the light, And now it weeps on misery flung; Now it mourns, now it thrills with joy; Now it wails, now it hears its doom; Now it hears its doom, now it dies, And now it leaves us, never to return.
It, hapless straying, treads the maze of ills.
But Jesus said, Father, behold, A strife of ills across the earth Wanders from thy breath (of wrath); But bitter Chaos (man) seeks to shun, And knows not how to pass it through.
On this account, O Father, send me; Bearing seals, I shall descend; Through ages whole I'll sweep, All mysteries I'll unravel, And forms of Gods I'll show; And secrets of the saintly path, Styled "Gnosis," I'll impart." (The Gnostic Society Library)

This is the salvation story of man which is far from a condemnation story of women.

There are two translations of this text, the earlier test does not mention "she" at all but by the 19th century there she was and things for women could only get worse.

Egyptian God Re or Ra quote:

"...this Holy God, the Lord of all the gods or the Holy Soul who came into being in the beginning, the great God who lives upon truth, the first God of primeval time, the beginning through whom every other god has existence...the beginning whose birth is hidden, whose evolutions are manifold, whose growth is incomprehensible...traverser of eternity, the aged One who renews his youth, who possesses myriad of pairs of eyes, and innumerable pairs of ears..."

This description of God is almost identical to the Naassene Sermon and in Hindu accounts.

By labeling these references fabrications or derivatives of ancient pagan text, skeptics have tried to label all accounts of ancient manuscripts that acknowledge that the Divine Energy and the existence of Christ long before the Greek and Roman era as false by simply calling them Pagan, outside of Christian Thought.

In today's world we simply say something like "God know all, see all, hears all and is the Alpha and the Omega, and the mass population is satisfied with that explanation, after about the third grade of school, because of living in a society that absolutely does not question religion.

Definition: Origin

The point at which something comes into existence, or from which it derives, or is derived, the fact of originating; rise or derivation.

Rise, beginning, or derivation from a source

It is the starting point. On a number line it is 0. On a two-dimensional graph it is where the Y axis and Y axis cross, marked (0,0).

A primary source, the original people that were created for life in the Garden of Eden of Earth came from the primary source.

The beginning of something; first stage; the origin of people does indeed go along with the "in the beginning story", but it is also the beginning part, that was left out of the retelling.

Ancestry is parentage, birth, extraction, all of these are explanations for what we do not know, the how, when, and what methods were used to create the first humans.

In math it can be explained as the point whose coordinates are all zero (0,0).

Definition: Admixture

A mixture; the action of adding an ingredient to something else; something formed by mixing

These four definitions have everything to do with what this book is all about. There are no accidents in the universe and there is an alpha point and an omega point, but then there is everything in-between.

In my search to dig deeper into the root system of the tree where knowledge is buried, these words were highlighted by the *Thoughtland*. Now the pieces have fallen into place.

While heaven and earth were still accessible for all inhabitants and while there was still a Jacob's ladder to climb, it was during the starting point and it was the origin of the first generation, the generation from source; the originals; the pure, unadulterated spirit beings of the Most High God.

The Gnostics call them the begotten as if to distinguish them from what came next, and as it turns out it is a very important distinction.

Definition: Begotten

Past participle of beget; as a noun to bring forth;
Ephesians 1:5 states *"he predestined us for adoption as sons through Jesus Christ, according to the purpose of his will"*

In John 3:16 it reads that God gave his only begotten son and again in Hebrews it reads that Abraham offered up his only son although he had other sons.

There is a need for discernment here about who can be begotten. It is not possible for me to reconcile the term" only begotten son" with Ephesians 1:5 where it clearly states that he predestined "us" which all happened before the foundation of the world. How did everything get boiled down from "us" to "only begotten son"? Not only that, but who decided that today's bible should read that the only begotten is of the father, while the divine mother is never mentioned. Yet, obscurely placed is the telling evidence, which belied and negates everything in the one statement by Jesus the Christ on the Cross of "Behold your Mother." If he was truly the only begotten child of the father wouldn't he have said behold your father? And just so we are clear he was talking to the other children of the Most High at the time. This statement was not to the masses as clergy would now have you to believe; for not everyone was begotten and not everyone shared the same divine nature of the mother.

Conclusions Drawn

Therefore, I contend that the *Children of the Light* came into being as the *first begotten* of the *Divine Mother* and were *the Zero point* and the *origin* of the royal bloodline, immortal in every respect and able to be raptured, incarnated, reincarnated and enjoy rest and repose.

Because of this very fact they are the most feared beings on the planet by those who know of their existence, due to the fact they possess the greatest inheritance that can be given, and it is the reason that the powerful of earth search for the foundation of youth, fear death and seek to make abortions of any sort illegal. There is no desire for that life once born, but they are seeking a savior to deliver them from what is coming, and they falsely assume that their savior will come in the form of a little baby.

I think they drank the Kool-Aid of lies and deception. A pure heart is the only way, there is no silver bullet; there is no magic pill; there is no instant savior, or "I've got plenty of time" to do whatever it is that I want to do and still have time to get right, or amass enough to buy my way in, for the truth is either you will fit through the eye of the needle or you will not.

While, they may have taken the earthly inheritance from the Children of the Light, they could not possess the most precious of gifts the Grace of everlasting life from the Divinity of the Mother.

When the earth is your power base and the ground is your resting place you are a mortal being and heaven is not your ever-after destination.

It was imperative this truth not come out and it was the job of the bible to hide this truth from those born from the ground of earth.

They were and still are carefully taught that their reward would come in heaven, while, those telling them this, were and are busy amassing their wealth in the here and now, because they have always known the truth. When you really look at mega churches today, where some pastors have amassed millions of dollars in personal tax free wealth from the poor, you begin to see the injustice and the deception. If their religion was so good for all, it would certainly have trickled down by now, all of these thousands of year's letter.

The only saving grace for the masses is the creation of a heart as light as a feather. One that is free of the karma of:

- Pride
- Greed
- Lust

- Malicious envy
- Gluttony
- Wrath
- Sloth
- ...and is immersed in the seven virtues of:
- Humility against pride
- Kindness against envy
- Abstinence against gluttony
- Chastity against lust
- Patience against anger
- Liberality against greed
- Diligence against sloth

But even if this is accomplished, without recognition of the Divine Mother, one still will not get through the eye of the needle, until ones calls upon the Mother and recognizes the source of all there is, was, and ever will be, to gain entrance into the kingdoms of heaven.

The bible can be the biggest deception tool, or the greatest inspirational device. It is all in how you choose to use it. If you choose to see it as pure gospel, just as it has been rewritten hundreds if not thousands of times, you will walk one way through life, but if you choose to see it as a tool to further your spiritual understanding, you will indeed open up to an entirely different way of learning through the bible. You will genuinely seek, grow and learn all there is to know about your connection to the Divine. The bible, as a resource, will serve you well and you will help you grow in Divine Grace.

There are Lords of the under realms and they demand allegiance and are ready to fight for their right to dominate, and they do not want you to dig deeper or to understand on a deeper level. Knowledge is their sworn enemy and for them hidden things should stay hidden. I am here to shine light on hidden things.

The seeds are planted and the coming time is approaching for all saints and all would be saints to get ready to raise the earth out of the depths of despair. This is a clarion call!

In Summation

It is summation time. By a preponderance of the evidence I have tried to establish enough information to prove my premise, that the bible is only a guide to knowledge, but not the whole and complete foundation of knowledge. It is not the Encyclopedia Britannica of my childhood, but a spiritual guide, which one has to view through spiritual eyes. There are lines between the lines and cracks in every verse, every psalm, every parable, every proverb, and in every character. The book was written as a lay story for the masses and as a research book for the enlightened. The lay people were to be kept in the dark, while the enlightened were fed the food that sustains life and props up the powerful.

In doing so, a valuable truth had to be hidden, which changed everything from the beginning to today.

Who is the Holy Spirit, the Divine Mother, why do we have the iconic Mother and Child, yet there is only the Father, the Son and the Male Holy Spirit?

Why hasn't anyone told their congregation that Genesis Chapter One took place in the spiritual realm and that when it talked about making man in their image, it only meant with their divine nature?

Why didn't anyone tell their congregation that Genesis Chapter Two took place in the earthly realm and when it talked about forming man from the ground it took material that was in the earthly realm to help form the future evolution of humans?

Why weren't we allowed to know that there were actually two separate and distinctly different types of humanity in existence?

The definitions of *zero point*, *origin*, and *begotten* are critical in that they pertain only to the first beings the ones created in Genesis Chapter One.

Whereas the definition of *admixture* is the identifier of those formed from the ground in Genesis Chapter Two.

It is at this point that we can look no further than to the bible for the answer. The bible had a lot to say about the blood and it turns out that there was a great deal hidden within the distorted information written in the bible to explain the importance of everything pertaining to the blood.

But in Genesis it speaks of the four rivers that flowed out of the Garden of Eden which is the representation of the four major blood types of the world. What reading the bible does not tell you is that the four rivers flowing were during a time when the upper realms of the heavens were accessible to the Earth when it was known as the Garden of Eden. The four blood types flowed into the earth and the earth was seeded with the people of the beginning. It was before the four rivers flowed that they were told to keep with their own kind. At this point every one of the all four blood types, were negative of any proteins.

Those blood types are A, B, AB, and O. Each blood type existed in a pure state at one time but after the "fall" somewhere between Genesis Chapter One and Genesis Chapter Two there were major changes to life as we now know it. The "fall" amounts to being disobedient and not keeping with one's own kind. I was another way of saying some did not stay in accordance with ones' divine nature, but however it was said, it caused great changes between the heavens and the earthly realm.

The four rivers that flowed out of Eden and all over the known world, was not without unintended consequences.

The bible speaks of the dangers of the mixing of the bloodlines but speaks of it in generic terms that seem reasonable when put in context of family tribes. But it also spoke, at one point, about keeping to one's own kind, and still no one thought anything of the warning, but it was very ominous, and did lead to dire consequences in terms of what was unleashed into the world through certain admixtures.

What was not clear was that through it all there was one type that remained unadulterated, pure, true to its origin, and unpenetrated and that was blood type O. But it wasn't just blood type O it was blood type O negative of the sealed variety, which medical science has called the blood type of unknown origin. How can this be? They have determined where every other blood type came from by being able to reproduce it. They have studied every other blood type and know everything about it. But no one can reproduce O negative. Some scientist have stated that it must be an anomaly because it just seems to show up unannounced, without anything that relates to a logical explanation, that can be scientifically proven.

This is something to ponder 0+0=0, correct? It makes sense that is the true Zero Point. A report came out and I admit I had never heard it before and didn't know if I believed it on its value.

The report stated that two people of blood type O negative cannot reproduce. I have no idea why I thought this was questionable at the time.

Of course it is true. If they could reproduce, there would be no mystery. We would know where the origin of O negative came from, and the greatest mystery of all time would have never taken place.

The mystery of God is awesome in that, all the scientist in the world cannot tell you how the original offspring of God continues to come into being.

The bible revealed the secrets, but man decided that those secrets pertained to time and space, and not to the spiritual or heavenly realms.

If something is chosen, selected, elected by the Most High God, it has already been identified.

If something is sealed by the Most High God, it cannot be tampered with.

If something is incarnated or reincarnated it will only seem to be random or an anomaly.

Therefore the four major blood groups in their purest state were all negative of any substance pertaining to the earth realm. However, all but blood type O negative could be manipulated and were subjected to be mixed, mingled, replicated and analyzed.

Human blood types are inherited and contain genetic contributions from each parent. When a blood type is said to be unknown it means, that neither the father, nor the mother contributed to the blood type in question. Since the parents didn't contribute and the offspring didn't inherit from them the offspring is said to be a true anomaly.

There is a chart that is very telling about the major blood types and their relationship to each other that continues to provide insight to me every time I take the time to explore it.

If you look closely at the chart you will see exactly what I am talking about.

Blood Type Study Guide

Blood Type	Gives to or Can Donate to	Can Receive From
O+	O+, A+, B+, AB+	O+, O-
A+	A+, AB+	A+, A-, O+, O-
B+	B+, AB+	B+, B-, O+, O-
AB+	AB+	All blood types (universal receiver)
O-	All blood types (universal donor)	O-
A-	A-, A+, AB-, AB+	A-, O-
B-	B-, B+, AB-, AB+	B-, O-
AB-	AB-, AB+	AB-, A-, B-, O-

- Blood type O negative can give to any blood type which is why it is known as the universal donor, but can only receive O negative blood
- Blood type O positive can give to all positive blood types
- Blood type AB+ can only give to AB+, but can receive from all blood types which is why it is known as the universal receiver
- The rarest blood type is AB- because it has the smallest percentage in the population with AB+ doing on slightly better. AB+ has a saving grace, it is a universal receiver, a grace that AB- does not have.

Yet while percentage wise they are the rarest, O negative, while it is the universal donor can only receive from O negative which is just five to seven percent of the world's population.

But that isn't the only reason that O negative is in my opinion, the rarest blood type regardless of the numbers, it is the rarest because it is sealed and cannot be manipulated or tampered with by any of the known and unknown entities that have tried.

The fact that the largest concentration is in the United States and England is also a fact to keep in mind as we approach the coming events of the future. Why would so many sealed beings be drawn to reincarnate in the Western power grid?

Blood!

Chapter Thirteen

Blood of Unknown Origin

What these charts show you is, that the *Blood of Unknown Origin* as it is sometimes called, was at one time pure unadulterated and free from any earthly sources, which they have not been able to explain. This blood type has been bombarded with scientific medaling, and changes have occurred but it still remains a universal donor to all other blood types.

And although a blood type O negative can donate blood to another O negative person two O negative people cannot reproduce, which is why, it is call blood of unknown origin.

If it wasn't for the story of Mary and the Immaculate Conception I would never have been able to solve the mystery in my own mind. But with the help of Mother Mary, I've reached the conclusion, that the anomaly is what the bible calls the *Immaculate Conception*. The result of this conception is called the incarnation or reincarnation by Gnostics and Spiritualist, and it happens more frequently than what we are told. We were only told about one of the occurrences of the Immaculate Conception, when it happened to the Christ. In the case of the high priest Melchizedek, his birth is simply recorded as being fatherless and motherless. It turns out that it is just possibly not quite the anomaly it was thought to be. I have finally connected these dots for myself and to my understanding and now I am sharing them with you.

The bible really didn't want to talk much about Melchizedek at all, but seeing that he was the original Christ, High Priest forever, it seems that he might be the one that keeps getting incarnated to offer up salvation from time to time, dispensation to dispensation.

I'm thinking roughly about five to seven percent of the world's population can claim to come here by way of an immaculate conception, incarnation or an reincarnation from the beginning of the creation of the originals.

It is said that the world's population of blood type O negative is 7 percent, which means that 93 percent of the population is not sealed, chosen, elected and set aside, but for what purpose I have to ask?

The presence of O negative blood type is a great help to human existence because with the passage of time, there have been so many variables entered into the blood supply chain which has made blood matching more and more complicated, but O negative has remained a constant as a universal source.

The fact that about 45 percent of Caucasians are Type O; whereas 57 percent of Hispanics are Type O, and 51 percent of African Americans are Type O, tells us of the inter-dependence there is on Type O for survival. It is a blood supply that is constantly in demand and thereby always in short supply.

Here are some additional facts I gathered from my research:
- Genetic studies find that all creatures can only inherit what their ancestors had with the exception of the mutation which would be the case with man and ape
- Blood factors are the most accurate to determine ancestry
- Eighty-five percent of humans have a blood factor common with the rhesus monkey's positive blood type
- All primates on earth have the same Rh factor
- Rh positive humankind and all primates come from common earthly ancestors

The word blood is mentioned more than any other word in the bible other than God. Why hasn't the scientific community questioned the absence of the Rh factor in greater detail in lay circles, why isn't it commonly known? Since there does not seem to be any earthly connection, where and what is the blood connected too?

So the question, genetics have continued to be perplexed about is where did Rh-negative come from, or are they?

If scientist want to prove that humankind is a hybrid and the missing link, as some suggest, that is fine with me. I personally am not in the same school of thought. I just want to know who and where the blood of unknown origin came from and what else is associated with this unknown blood type.

I have never understood the statement the biblical Jesus made in John 10:30, *"I and the Father are one."* I should have looked for the deeper meaning and not just assumed that the explanation I was given was correct, or the hyperbole of the scribes.

Could it be as simple as they were cut from the same cloth? Come out of the same dye? And was the Wedding Feast story in the bible yet another insight to how the process of being a child of the Most High God, one cut from the same cloth, out of the same dye, comes into the fullness of their being.

Are the verses in Ecclesiastes 3:1-8 concerning a time for everything appreciative of these times, that Jesus spoke of them, when he said something to the effect, that it was not time? Is there so much more coming, than just the small signs and wonders, we will be capable of performing? Should we not waste it on the small things in life to impress those attending the feast, but save it for those accepting the marriage? For it is said, "theirs is the kingdom of heaven", which is the big stuff.

The bible is a fascinating book. It cannot and should never be taken lightly or non-spiritually. Our continued growth and evolution depend entirely in our spiritual awareness and the bible in the western hemisphere has become for far too many, the only source, for a connection with the Most High God, but tragically its full power has been suppressed.

For your consideration, do you remember how excited the Christian world was to learn of the Shroud of Turin over 117 years ago? Could it be that they were hoping to find out the blood type of the Christ? It was reported that there were bloodstains but we have never heard anything about a blood study report or any finding.

Oh, here is another, in my mind these all are starting to fit together somehow. The term "blood brothers" which is a Native American term seems relevant here, as it is a much easier way to tell if you are kin. The two would cut and mingle their blood. If the blood clumped, you were not related. It was an earlier blood test for Rh-negative and Rh-positive blood typing, neat right? But the question is not about the blood but what they blood test could tell them. Are you from the stars or are you from the earth? The Native Americans were and still are very spiritual people and they would not share everything with just anyone. The test was necessary to determine who to share what with.

The ancients have always wanted the genealogy to be preserved, from Genesis forward. In caves on quilts down through the ages bloodlines have been recorded. Today there is a big push to identify where you came from and to what group you belong. Get a DNA test, find your ancestors, it all sounds well and good, but in the back of my mind; I am not completely convinced that there is not some nefarious plot in the mix of this knowledge.

Matthew 10:16 *"...be wise as serpents...!"*

Tinkering with the Blood

I long ago determined that the blood was the subject of many studies and some of them were indeed biblical in nature.

Why does infant Hemolytic disease occur in humans if all humans are of the same species? It initially occurred when an Rh negative mother is carrying an Rh positive child. But now the gene has been passed down from generation to generation in a hereditary.

This does not occur with other animal creatures with the exception of the mule which is a hybrid of a horse and donkey.
There is also the subject of Sickle Cell Anemia and thalassemia which are blood disorders which is also hereditary.

You never know what is true, but somewhere between six thousand blood factors and five hundred known blood proteins make up the humankind family of people existing on the planet today. That is a lot of variation and a lot of deviation from where we originally came from.

So between the animal wonder lust, alien intervention and mad scientist searching for a better species, one has to wonder if any or all of these contributed to the thousands of variations we have on the planet today.

We also have to ask if all of this infusion of various different elements has caused the chaotic strife we see in the world. Can it simply be that there are reasons why we don't seem to be able to come together on one accord? Is it indeed in need of divine intervention from a higher power?
You cannot begin to imagine my excitement upon learning about Heneritta Lacks and the missing link in my research.

My theory of the immortal bloodline is true beyond a shadow of a doubt even if it only means, I am on to something. Can you imagine we have a human immortal cell, a cell that does not die, one that lives on outside of the host body?

Now, let's be perfectly honest, if there is one Heneritta Lacks, there are more, and if they found one, they are looking for more, and if they find another, they will do the same thing steal the cells.

Re-Knowing the Origins

Chapter Fourteen

Re-knowing the Origins

Could it be the most important role in history?

The Book of Revelation and the Children of Unknown Origin!

One important thing to note is that while the O negative blood type is sealed it is also accessible as a universal donor. This will probably become very important at some point because there are no coincidences in the universe and everything has a season of planting and a season of harvesting.

Revelation 144,000

The bible also speaks in Revelation of the *144,000*. The number is very important and relates to the coming end of the dispensation period and the new beginning which comes at the end of every age. What the 144,000 does not represent is a real number, but a symbolic representation so we must look at what it means symbolically, such as 1+4+4 = 9 and 9 represents a complete gestation period the end of the pregnancy period; the end of a regulation baseball game and at the end Revelations states that all the saints will come and do battle. Now the biblical Revelations:

Revelation 14 (KJV)
14 *And I looked, and, lo, a Lamb stood on the mount Sion, and with him an hundred forty and four thousand, having his Father's name written in their foreheads.*
2 And I heard a voice from heaven, as the voice of many waters, and as the voice of a great thunder: and I heard the voice of harpers harping with their harps:
3 And they sung as it were a new song before the throne, and before the four beasts, and the elders: and no man could learn that song but the hundred and forty and four thousand, which were redeemed from the earth.

They had ears to hear
4 These are they which were not defiled with women; for they are virgins. These are they which follow the Lamb whithersoever he goeth. These were redeemed from among men, being the firstfruits unto God and to the Lamb.

The sealed, the chosen, the elected, the blood type O negative

⁵ *And in their mouth was found no guile: for they are without fault before the throne of God.*

Having been found faultless in Ephesians

⁶ *And I saw another angel fly in the midst of heaven, having the everlasting gospel to preach unto them that dwell on the earth, and to every nation, and kindred, and tongue, and people,*

⁷ *Saying with a loud voice, Fear God, and give glory to him; for the hour of his judgment is come: and worship him that made heaven, and earth, and the sea, and the fountains of waters.*

⁸ *And there followed another angel, saying, Babylon is fallen, is fallen, that great city, because she made all nations drink of the wine of the wrath of her fornication.*

Notice here, how evil is always represented as a woman

⁹ *And the third angel followed them, saying with a loud voice, If any man worship the beast and his image, and receive his mark in his forehead, or in his hand,*

Wait, hold up, didn't verse one just say they had the name of God on their forehead?

¹⁰ *The same shall drink of the wine of the wrath of God, which is poured out without mixture into the cup of his indignation; and he shall be tormented with fire and brimstone in the presence of the holy angels, and in the presence of the Lamb:*

Without mixture?? While I do not understand this, I do know it is important

¹¹ *And the smoke of their torment ascendeth up forever and ever: and they have no rest day nor night, who worship the beast and his image, and whosoever receiveth the mark of his name.*

Still confused about the mark of his name on the forehead

¹² *Here is the patience of the saints: here are they that keep the commandments of God, and the faith of Jesus.*

¹³ *And I heard a voice from heaven saying unto me, Write, Blessed are the dead which die in the Lord from henceforth: Yea, saith the Spirit, that they may rest from their labours; and their works do follow them.*

¹⁴ *And I looked, and behold a white cloud, and upon the cloud one sat like unto the Son of man, having on his head a golden crown, and in his hand a sharp sickle.*

¹⁵ *And another angel came out of the temple, crying with a loud voice to him that sat on the cloud, Thrust in thy sickle, and reap: for the time is come for thee to reap; for the harvest of the earth is ripe.*

¹⁶ *And he that sat on the cloud thrust in his sickle on the earth; and the earth was reaped.*

17 And another angel came out of the temple which is in heaven, he also having a sharp sickle.
18 And another angel came out from the altar, which had power over fire; and cried with a loud cry to him that had the sharp sickle, saying, Thrust in thy sharp sickle, and gather the clusters of the vine of the earth; for her grapes are fully ripe.
19 And the angel thrust in his sickle into the earth, and gathered the vine of the earth, and cast it into the great winepress of the wrath of God.

<u>Vine of the earth here, may be referring to those formed of the earth</u>
20 And the winepress was trodden without the city, and blood came out of the winepress, even unto the horse bridles, by the space of a thousand and six hundred furlongs.

Shedding Light on the Tower of Babel

There was a time when all beings in the spiritual realm spoke the same language. It was the language of Love given to them by the Divine Mother. Then there came a time when some of the beings (children) wanted to ascend above their station of existence, and hence we have the story of the Tower of Babel. The first time the story was told, it was not about something that happened in the physical realm, but what happened in the heavenly realm.

This is what caused the striking down and the descent into the earthly realms. This is what caused the confusion of tongues, or the different discordant energies of the new blood types as the end of their divine spiritual nature and compatibility with all things heavenly and the Divine Mother.

Everything that occurred thereafter with the injection of at least 29 different blood types, of every known origin, all with different tongues (spirit energies) all foreign to the Most High God, have one thing in common. They have nothing to do with an actual tower.

History and the bible have tried to come into sync with story after story and geography location after location, to no avail. Well there is very good reasons for not being able to do so. The geography of the world changed, continents disappeared, and continents appeared, land mass connections disappeared and land mass connections appeared. The land mass of the biblical history of the last 6 thousand years is not the same as what existed 50 to 100 thousand years ago.

Looking for a Tower of Babel, or finding a Noah's Ark, or locating the Lost City of Atlantis are not things we are probably going to find, for when you seek to find something that could have occurred 100 thousand years ago and fit it into a 6 thousand year time frame. How could you ever hope to find it, especially when you are looking in all the wrong places to begin with?

But the most important thing is when you, because of your upbringing and teachings or indoctrination are still under the impression that there is something you can physically do to change the outcome of the judgment to come. This completely misses the point of repenting and asking for redemption from the only one who can actually give it. The inward work one needs to do, can never be replaced by outward works.

The Angels were told...

It is said in the bible, that the Angels looked upon the daughters of men and saw that they were fair. It is also said that they were warned to stay with their own kind. We now know that this did not happen. The angels did not stay with their own kind since the population grew into a Rhesus Monkey positive group of humans and Eve became the mother with the determinant gene.

I don't blame the bible for whitewashing this truth, but the evidence does speak for itself. They simply disobeyed a known law.

It turns out there are logical reasons for doing so. They simply could not stay with their own kind and reproduce for they could not reproduce and create the population needed to till the soil and grow the food and build the things, that their spiritual abilities had once so easily accomplished, and they were quickly losing their abilities as they descended further and further away from the spiritual realms into the density of earth.

Remember it is recorded that their lifespan started to decline, from when there was a time they enjoyed very long lifespan, of eight to nine hundred years as recorded in the bible, but their RH positive off-springs only were soon maxed out at 120 years.

There is also the Sari and Abraim example of not being able to conceive and reproduce the nations promised by Melchizedek. Ask me if I really think that the high priest Melchizedek would have actually said this, but it makes for bringing legitimacy to a point of view you are trying to make. I always believed it until somewhere in this journey, it didn't make sense.

Anyway Abraim was told to lay with their servant and he did and the servant became pregnant and he became the father of many nations.

But, if this is where the rhesus monkey gene came from, then who was it exactly that told Sari to tell Abraim to sleep with a monkey? Are you seeing how this story doesn't make sense? It made perfect sense six thousand years ago, but a hundred thousand years ago when it was just your tribe unable to conceive and the rhesus monkey, it is not making for a good storyline. It is however a good enough story for the masses. It explains nothing but gives them the ability to move on and not question it or dig any deeper.

However, if there was no prejudice between the species, back in those days around a hundred thousand years ago then maybe it did naturally occur. But the bible states that each should stay with their own kind. Which kind was the bible referring too? Was it possible that it was the different blood types should not mingle, foretelling what would occur if the blood types intermingled from a genetic standpoint. There are great unanswered questions here and much food for thought. I leave you with them.

I am not one of the masses anymore, and that is why there are flags everywhere.

I have to my satisfaction identified the Blood of Unknown Origin as belonging to the elected, chosen, and sealed, children of the Most High God. These children having been brought into existence from the zero point of human creation before the foundation of the world, meaning they inherited nothing from the earth they now inhabit, but were born motherless and fatherless and made for the sole purpose of the Most High God. No one can command them; no one else can control them, and no one else will ever know their comings and their goings.

They belong to the Most High God and answer only to the Most High God, even if they themselves do not know it yet.

The Most High God

Most High God – you answer to only the highest God, there are many little gods, and other want to be gods, but the children of the Light answer only to the Most High God and should only use this terminology to describe their allegiance. This mistake has been made by many people who end swearing allegiance to demi-gods such as described in the Old Testament. There are many wrong or misinterpretations of the Most High God that are deliberately designed to confuse and sway you. There are many ways people have decided to describe God, which have become very acceptable over time. Do not use them. Lord is not an acceptable term for the Most High God, neither is God, since the sound of God or god sound the same as it is resonated out in the ethers. For instance, you may call your significant other, "Boo", or "honey", or "dear", but in a legal document or in a court of law only the legal title can be placed in the document of record. It is the same with those who have entered into a contract with the Most High God. Your contract is with the Most High and only the Most High. To call upon anyone else will not get your contract honored, but make no mistake, you are so valuable to God, that many other gods will answer your call and try to convince you they are the real thing.

We are all Children

We are the children, we are all the children, some from the original seed and some from the admixture, but we all reside here on the earth from time to time.

We all have opportunities to grow, learn and evolve. The choice to sink further into the lower realms of existence is also a choice, and undoubtedly some will take the path of least resistance, but that too is their choice.

The clarion call is coming soon, and all will answer it for none are immune from the call. All will be drawn to its sound, and none will escape their ultimate fate.

The human spirit is a true barometer of everything that lies within the body. The human Chakra System contains the memory of the outcome of all actions and reactions; as well as every thought and every deed. When the Chakra System is seen with the spiritual eye the individual's evolution is quite visible and the story of their journey of evolution becomes evident.

The bible talks about the seven churches and their attributes which is right in line with the seven chakras of the human body. We are the church, remember the words of The Christ, "suffer the little children to come unto me."

It was well known that there were different evolutionary paths and that there were humans on the earth traveling those different paths. We are still traveling in different paths, different circles and have different goals and agendas.

There are over six hundred antigens found on the surface of different blood cells showing how far from the original source some have strayed. These differences have led to many birth defects and disorders in the general population resulting in diseases that was never known in the heavenly realm.

But children remember you are not a missing link. You have never been lost. In fact you have always been linked to the Most High God. The Most High God is your refuge and your strength in all times of great joy and great sorrow. You need never be afraid, for you are never alone. No matter how low you sink or how high you rise you are never alone.

Fear not!

Worry not, for troubled waters lead to calm seas.

Dig
Before the calm there is a storm,
we are in the midst of the storm.
Our way out, lies in the roots of symbolism,
it runs deep!
We must continue to dig past the indoctrination
of carefully taught fear,
Our arrival at our true destination depends on it.

Chapter Fifteen

The Continued Need for Fear

Divine Energy is attracted to the nature of your divine spirit, as expressed in the fruits of the spirit of love, joy, peace, longsuffering, gentleness, goodness and above all faith, when these are emitted into the atmosphere, the universe responds and correspondence begins between the loved and the beloved. Galatians 5:22 (KJV)

Therefore the creation of fear was necessary. I call it the Great Transference of Fear. It still exists today and has caused divisions, which have led to all of the wars from the very beginning to the wars raging in our world today.

At some time in our thinking, we are called upon to consider the masculine nature of the earthly realm.

Lord is a masculine title.

The earth age after the flood was under a masculine influence which replaced the influence of the Heavenly Holy Spirit.

On earth you had:

- LORDS
- Lords
- gods
- Kings
- Princes

These were the titles given to your new leaders, and the list of titles only grew as new additional masculine leader emerged. Each rebellion gave power to new leaders; each conquest of land brought others into servitude and the rise of masculine might and force reigned supreme on the vast majority of the earthly plane.

A rebellion between might and right is a repeated theme throughout the ages, as right struggles to remain relevant from the beginning to now.

It was the rebellion from the beginning that necessitated the creation of fear.

The story of Sodom and Gomorrah is for me at the center of its creation.

Even before I got to the Sodom and Gomorrah story in the bible, there were bells and whistles going off at the very mention of Lot leaving with Sari and Abriam. For some reason which was not clear to me at the time, Lot seemed really out of order, and in the wrong place. He just didn't fit into the narrative in which he was supposed to fit.

By this time I had become accustomed to the flags that offered more questions than answers, so yet another question was placed on the shelf in my brain. Lot was indeed a puzzle that continued to nag at me from time to time.

I had already learned to think that nothing of the literal interpretation of the bible was gospel, so my mind kept being inquisitive about Lot and later even more so with his connection to Sodom and Gomorrah.

The pairing of Two's are very important and very prominent in the bible which made it very odd to have Sari and Abriam, being told by the High Priest Melchizedek that they would leave the Garden of Eden and become the parents of many nations, only to have them go off with Lot. It is important to notice that the High Priest did not mention Lot or what his role would be in nation building. Yet, here they were going off into a strange land, and we are left clueless as to who this person was, or why he was chosen to be with them. This was a major biblical event and to this day historians still cannot get the relationship between Abriam and Lot straight, some say it is his brother, while other say he is his nephew or cousin, I err of the side of the place holder.

Just as the two's are an important number in the bible, three is a very important number in the bible and Lot, Sodom and Gomorrah do not a trinity make, for three was strictly reserved for the purpose of the Trinity. Since the bible's foundation is built on symbolism, it placed Lot once again out of order, making it all the more important, for there are no accidents in the universe, only better questions.

All of these questions came about before I had the insight of the *Thoughtland* at my disposal.

The bible itself was written on seven different levels that I could think of and maybe more, so looking strictly at the meaning of Lot's name gave meaning and understanding as to why the placement of Lot with Abriam and Sari was important to be there.

Lot means veil or covering, in the bible it is the veil that separates one from God, just as it does in the symbolic representation, of the inner structure, of the Ark of the Covenant.

Therefore, by placing Lot behind Sari and Abraim as they left the Garden of Eden, Lot represented not a person but the veil of separation between God and those who rebelled in some way against the heavenly realms.

I also want to point out that it is quite telling that because of the All Seeing Eye, Melchizedek was able to relay their future of being the parents of many nations.
It is also clear why the bible tells Abraim that he will be the father of many nations, I always include Sari as a parent, even though the bible does not. There are a few facts still just out of view, which may become clear later.

There are two additional things about Lot's appearance that are really noteworthy. First there is the destruction of Sodom and Gomorrah a city filled with sin and Homosexual acts and lazy greedy women according to the biblical stories.
Are we to believe that these two things were enough for "God" to bring destruction to an entire city? In what religion is it ever possible to place God in such an unloving vengeful demeanor?

If God could do this then surely The Christ would have done it as well. Surely he would have shown no mercy on those that whipped him, pierced his sides, stripped him of his clothes, gambled to see who would win them, or those that gave him bitter herbs to drink, or placed thorns on his head, surely they would have had the wrath of God rain down on them in an instant. Isn't that what vengeful gods do.

The second important Lot connected story is the symbolism of Lot seeing his wife turned into a pillar of salt which would have struck fear in anyone and did strike fear into all that longs to return to the heavenly realm and leave this earthly place that had not lived up to the hype.

By offering up Homosexuality and lazy greedy women as reasons for the downfall of Sodom and Gomorrah, it was then, the same as it today, a very convenient scapegoat.

The actors behind the scenes the Lords, Kings and clergy all conspired to instill *fear* and as control mechanism while at the same time laying blame squarely at the feet of others.

I keep sensing a certain willingness to blame women in the bible for all the woes, wrongs, and downfalls of man, with absolutely no regard for their part in bring themselves down. Why is it always a cry of "she did it to poor little me" being uttered by some burly built, sword carrying man? I know this is a delicate subject, but it is still a fair question to ask.

I think Lot's wife, real or imagined for the sake of the story, was sorry that she ever listen and was led from heaven, and how she felt was symbolic of so many that went on the journey by turning her into a pillar of salt was a lesson because now they know there is no returning back.

The ultimate weapon *fear* is one that keeps you in a self-imposed prison. But what is the motivator that makes us do it, why it's called Hell.

Hell is that place, were fire and brimstone lives, and where it is ground-hog day every day. No one wants to go there, so we try desperately to follow the thousands of do's and don'ts of the church, as well as the thousands other laws heaped on us by the central government, only managing to live in constant fear, that it is only a matter of time, when either the church or the government will find of us guilty of something. Judgment Day becomes a very scary proposition, which has some opting for the "live now and die young" attitude because they don't see a way out of the incarceration of their mind.

Hell was sold to us as a real place. It was called many things in the bible from a lake of fire, to Sheol, Hades, Tartarus, and Gehenna. There are several bibles that list the word "Hell" numerous times

The Latin Vulgate references it 110 and all of the King James Versions references it from 54 to 32 times, Holman Christian Standard Bible, while some others do not mention it at all, such as Young's, Twentieth Century New Testament, Rotherham's Emphasized Bible, Weymouth's Testament, Jewish Publication Society Bible OT, Emphatic Dialott Greek/English Int. or the Tamakh The Complete Jewish Bible.

Hell seems to have a very special place in the western bibles and in their teachings. It also seems to leave very little wiggle room for the sinners or the trying. But it is not "Hell" that should get the bad rap; it is just a mind construct, which we the people have adopted as our own personal bottomless pit, which at any second might swallow us up.

The creation of fear is firmly embedded in our lives. There are triggers everywhere, we are afraid of just about everything today. The fear mongers have either done or said things that keep us afraid of something at all times, such as:

- The air we breathe is poisonous with pollutants from Chemtrails
- The water is polluted with poisons, garbage, sharks, and now alligators
- That people of different colors are taking your food, water, jobs and they've come the rob, rape and kill you
- The government is ripping you off
- Wall Street is ripping you off
- Main Street is ripping you off
- Your representative are ripping you off

But did you ever notice, no one has ever said your traditional church is ripping you off, because they are not giving you the whole truth, and nothing but the whole truth about you and your relationship to the Most High God is what the church should be teaching you?

Their sole purpose should be to save souls, but not from hell fire and brimstone but to help you recognize your relationship with the Most High God, which will lead you upward and onward through your personal relationship, a relationship that doesn't require the church's intervention at every step, but one that is cultivated daily and is nourished 24/7/365!

If this has not been your experience, you should bring it to their attention. I was always afraid to say, that the teachings of the church are not satisfying for my spirit, but I implore you to not be like me. It took searching for forty years to get my courage up enough to seek, and ask and never be satisfied with less than the truth. Don't be like me, start now, and ask about everything you ever wanted to know. A good church at heart will endeavor to find your answers. You will know if it is a good church soon enough.

What you have to gain is a personal relationship that will leave you rewarded and better off for it. One in which allows you to enjoy happiness on earth, instead of waiting for the "hereafter" or waiting for the "joy to come in the morning" or in the "bye and bye!" Having and maintaining a personal relationship with the Most High God would mean that you, and not the masses, are in control of your happiness and your Utopia is here on earth, and that your church attendance is not for your need for a mediator between you and God or for your salvation, but for fellowship with kindred spirits.

Phraseology: Pillar of Salt

During the course of looking closely at the story of Sodom and Gomorrah and what happened to the wife of Lot, I was gently nudged to ponder why she was turned into a pillar of salt and not say something else like just plain ashes?

My first thought was about the salt itself. I had thought salt was a very valuable commodity in those days. So I did some research and found my assumption to be true. It was highly valued in ancient times as a:

- Seasoning
- Disinfectant
- Preservative
- Used in ceremonial offerings
- Unit of exchange

The research also revealed that there were certain descriptions attributed to salt in those times such as:

- Permanence
- Loyalty

- Durability
- Fidelity
- Usefulness
- Purification

The bible states that an angel leads Lot out of Sodom and destroys the city. Could the story actually be about the 'fallen' angel leading the children out of heaven and the destruction of Sodom was really the destruction of the bridge or the gulf between heaven and earth?

Could Lot's wife represent those who had, had a change of heart who really espoused the attributes of the salt and wanted to return to heaven?

I am now looking at the story in a very different light. The Thoughtland never disappoints me. I am constantly amazed by new insight.

The following passages in the bible also help to shine a light on the use of salt. There are no accidents in the universe and no coincidences in the use or placement of words in the bible, even if the scribe doesn't understand the rhythm or reason the universe does.

"And every oblation of thy meat offering shalt thou season with salt; neither shalt thou suffer the salt of the covenant of thy God to be lacking from thy meat offering: with all thine offerings thou shalt offer salt." Leviticus 2:13 (KJV)
"And thou shalt offer them before the LORD, and the priests shall cast salt upon them, and they shall offer them up for a burnt offering unto the LORD." Ezekiel 43:24 (KJV)

These two verses confirm the value of salt in ceremonial burnt offerings which acknowledges and exalts their purification properties as well as their properties as a seasoning.

"All the heave offerings of the holy things, which the children of Israel offer unto the LORD, have I given thee, and thy sons and thy daughters with thee, by a statute for ever: it is a covenant of salt for ever before the LORD unto thee and to thy seed with thee." Numbers 18:19 (KJV)

This introduces a new covenant into the lexicon a salt covenant for those who were led out of Sodom, as a part of the exodus out of heaven. I am convinced these were a part of the biblical 'fallen'.

Salt is also described as a desolate no man's land when it is a land mass, but the same land mass has been used to harvest the valuable salt. It does show however the double edged sword and the continuing duality in the bible.

The fact that every time you look at something in the bible is a reason to keep reading it but without eyes to see and ears to hear, the truth may not easily flow and your ability to discern is completely dependent on your relationship with the Most High God.

One of my most important learning's was that no matter what I have gleaned it should not be tied to written absolutes or totally current thinking, for as new information comes into view old assumptions may change, for the universe has always explained what is immutable and what is not.

Keep Digging

Never stop digging for the root of things
all words and phrases in the Bible matter,
don't let them stay undeveloped in your mind.

Chapter Sixteen

The Deeper I go the Greater the Clarity

Definition: The Veil

In Hebrew it means the divider, the separator, something that hides. The veil is referenced in the Holy of Holies, the Ark of the Covenant, which is the physical representation of the separation between the heavenly and the earthly realm.

The only one allowed to enter is the high priest still only at appointed times by the Most High God. Any biblical reenactment is just that, for no one has accurately been able to pinpoint the exact time of the return of the most high priest or as Christians call The Christ.

The Veil is very important to our understanding of where we are and where God is. The Most High God is beyond the veil. We are on the other side and it is only through meditation, pray, a willingness to be still, and to know, that the power to connect resides in the intrinsic nature of the universe itself. Everything we need, to do so, is indeed here, we are not disconnected for it is us that have silenced our voice through lack of knowledge and lack of use. The veil is there as a filter, but those who can go through the narrow gate, or through the eye of the needle, or who's heart is as light as a feather will have easy access to enter at the appointed time.

The most important take-away for me is that the veil that divides us from the Most High God, does not divide the Most High God from us.

The story, of which we will never know the true origin of or the true placement in time and space, talks about how the veil was torn in half, from the top to the bottom.

The significance of this statement bears looking at very closely. For being torn from top means to me that the action of tearing came from the heavens above and went all the way down to the ends of earth. Hallelujah! The Most High God is indeed in charge.

This would be a fundamental shift from what we have now; it would also mean that something monumental would have to occur to make us worthy of such reconciliation with the Most High God.

It would mean that the end of a dispensation occurred, and that a new era of togetherness was upon us. I say hallelujah in advance for such a time.

Therefore, while a Christ may appear in the Holy of Holies to help save us from time to time, it is only through the tearing of the veil completely that unites all people, and biblically this occurs at the end of Revelation in the bible.

Lot's wife looked back at the closed veil and saw the separation of humankind from the realms of the Most High God and for that the earthy powers render her to a pillar of salt. But I feel that the salt purified Lot's wife and her spirit and her spirit alone and returned to The Most High God.

In my opinion, all references to the veil are other worldly and not to be placed into time and space.

For far too long, we have let a lie get in the way of the truth that would set us free.

Phraseology: Formed versus Created

There is confusion in the bible as a whole and within the books themselves. A book that has always confused me and continues to do so is the Book of Isaiah. One wonders how something can be written by one author when the words used to denote a thing, or an occurrence is used differently by another or using very different terminologies, sometimes in the same book. And so it is with formed and created.

The difference between Genesis Chapter One and Genesis Chapter Two makes this quite apparent.

Now in Isaiah, which I am forever grateful for, because it validates what I said previously, look at this.
Thus says the LORD who made you and formed you from the womb, who will help you. Do not fear, O Jacob My servant; And you Jeshurun whom I have chosen.
Isaiah 44:2
"Thus says the LORD, the King of Israel, for you are My servant; I have formed you, you are My servant, O Israel, you will not be forgotten by Me."

Isaiah 44:21
But now thus said the LORD that created, O Jacob, and he that formed you, O Israel, Fear not: for I have redeemed you, I have called you by your name; you are mine.

Whether it is deliberate or an unintended error, it is misleading and misguided. It muddies the waters between reality and falsehood. It doesn't allow our discernment to have clarity.

The Most High God is a Creator God.

The LORD, ruler of Earth is a god who forms; he formed from the earth those that are loyal to him. He exalts those of his tribe, those he formed are those that belong to him in the earthly realms and as such, have not had access to the heavenly realms.

The conversation to the created came from the Christ, the redeemer, but has no association with the LORD, for they are indeed in opposite camps. However, the intermingling of thoughts leads to the confusion and acceptance that they are all the same. It is these very misleading passages in the Bible that has let the true Antichrist (negative energy) to flourish and thrive. The absoluteness of the gospel has become twisted it exists to serve two masters in its literal form.

I sometimes hear the incoherent messages coming out of churchgoers mouths as they try desperately to validate, hate, prejudice, and all manner of violence toward another group in the name of their god.

When the bible is read literally and where some text within it is in and of itself convoluted, weaker minds are easily persuaded to be guided a certain way in ways that would never have been in compliance with the original text.

The difference between being formed on earth and being created in heaven is just another phrase in the bible that should give us all cause to pause.

The Story of Elijah and Elisha

The story was always a wonderful story when told by pastors and ministers in churches time after time, never really deviating from the story I had first heard, but somehow it was yet another biblical story that I put on the shelf in my brain as something to ponder when I had the time. It was just a tad bit out of order.

I, just like everyone else always had a tendency to be stuck in the literal, and even when flags flew, I indeed looked for plausible literal answers. But if you look at Elijah as a symbolic representation of the Children of Light then the things surrounding Elijah take on a different meaning and one that gives plausible answers not just more questions.

The light goes on and just as Elijah is symbolic of the Children of the Light Elisha may be symbolic of the Children of the "fall".

The Children of the Fall wanted more than they were given they wanted to be like God, therefore they wanted more than the representative Elijah had, which is where the double portion came from.

The bible tells us it was Elijah that was taken up to heaven, not Elisha, and as writers of the bible insert a story very similar to the Moses story of striking the stone and lo and behold Elisha gets a double portion and goes to heaven too. However if Elisha truly could receive a double portion and if Elijah could truly give it to him, by whose authority was it possible and why was there never any mention of double portions anywhere else? Why did everyone else have to go through the eye of the needle, or through the narrow gate?

The whole problem is the asking for more than what Elijah, had a double portion. The justification rendered by scholars after the fact that it was like what is given to the firstborn is saying that Elijah had the ability to add names to the original book of life which he did not. Nor did Elijah redeem him and therefore was able to add him to the Lamb's Book of Life, unless Elijah was indeed the incarnation of the Christ. But the bible failed to mention that Elijah was an incarnation of the Christ of the Age. While at the same time giving him authorities like the Christ and granting him permission to add to the heavenly roles, while saving no one else. Isn't this just strange?
Wouldn't a much better biblical explanation, of how this was at all possible, have been helpful? Why is it hidden and seen as speculative knowledge? Why haven't the scholars cleared it up by now, surly they could?

This is another new found understanding about the duality found in the bible and the misconceptions duality has led too. These two also show the introduction of envy into the souls of beings, it is the things that wars are fought over and it may have been the first war that laid the foundation for all wars since. But it is also this enviable request that leads me to believe that Elisha was not taken up into heaven. I think it was man's wishful thinking.

To ponder: The trait of envy will get you thrown out or left out of heaven, therefore an enviable request will not get you back into heaven.

The Book of Life and the Lamb's Book of Life

There are two books in which the names of the Children are written which need explanation and a greater understanding. The Book of Life and the Lamb's Book are referenced in many verses, some I will share. The Lamb's book of Life is filled with names of people who lived in the earthly realm and were redeemed by the sacrifice of the Christ. Those who were washed by the blood, the redeemed of the world are written into the Lamb's Book of Life.

The Book of Life is a different book that names were added to before the foundation of the world for they were created before and given an inheritance of everlasting life before sin was ever a factor and redemption and sacrifice was ever needed.

Two different books, the Book of Life contains the names of the Children of Light, and the Lamb's Book of Life contains the Children of the Most High God. These are two distinct classifications because their missions in their various lives are different, and their intuitive natures may be different. Which is why, I am certain that there are two separate books. Some scholars would have you believe that there is only one book and that there is no distinction before the books or the names written therein.

This can't possibly be true, when one group is not corrupted by the original sin nature and the other group is and has to be redeemed of it. While one group received and inheritance before the foundation of the world and the other group did not. I don't see apples and apples, I see apples and oranges and wishful thinking.

The Book of Life bible passages:
And if anyone's name was not found written in the book of life, he was thrown into the lake of fire. Revelation 20:15
The one who conquers will be clothed thus in white garments, and I will never blot his name out of the book of life. I will confess his name before my Father and before his angels.
Revelation 3:5
And I saw the dead, great and small, standing before the throne, and books were opened. Then another book was opened, which is the book of life. And the dead were judged by what was written in the books, according to what they had done.
Revelation 20:12 (ESV)

This passage references the "books" and the Book of Life was singled out as being separate and apart from the others.
But now, if you will forgive their sin — but if not, please blot me out of your book that you have written." But the Lord said to Moses, "Whoever has sinned against me, I will blot out of my book. Exodus 32:32-33 (ESV)

The original exodus led the fallen out of the original Garden of Eden. In this passage Moses is asking that their names not be taken out of the Book, but the answer came back that their names were taken out. This is why there was a need to deploy a savior and to create another book. It was done to be able to add the fallen originals back in to the fold, through the lamb's Book of Life.

Some basic facts omitted
from the Bible
are paramount to your growth!

Chapter Seventeen

Man Made Laws verses Universal Laws (Spiritual Laws)

T his is one of the most important bits of hidden knowledge we
should have access to and an understanding thereof.
The system of checks and balances, does not just pertain to the laws
enacted by man, whether in the bible or through the governing bodies on
earth. There are other laws that govern our existence in ways not known
to far too many of us.

We cannot govern the world or ourselves effectively if we do not
understand the foundational laws upon which the planet we occupy is
based on. We cannot effect change, make good choices, adequately
prepare ourselves or have an effect our evolutionary progress, unless we
are aware of, and have knowledge of, the greater laws that exist for all on
an individual and collective basis.

There are laws that govern your cities, states, and your country,
break one of these laws and your individual freedom and/or finances may
be affected.

There are laws that govern your religion and your church break
any of these laws and the church will dole out punishment befitting a
sinner usually in the form of some sort of hell and damnation rhetoric,
usually delivered during a Sunday sermon in mild cases, for in Western
church lore, "We are all sinners and fall short of the grace of God."

In some religious sects the punishment may be excommunication
from the church for disobeying the tenants of the religion. When this
happens it is more about the religion itself and much less about the Most
High God's position on anything.

A God of love is a forgiving God, a loving God, and a God who
would not impose restrictions that impede growth, creativity and
compassion. We are here to learn and grow from our mistakes, not to be
punished for them on multiple levels of daily existence.

The Universal or Spiritual Laws that govern the entire universe are
different and some are Immutable and some are Mutable, knowing the
difference is just as important as knowing the existence of the laws
themselves.

There are three Immutable laws which means they are eternal, absolute and will never change until Earth and Heaven shall pass away as read in Revelation.

The three Immutable Laws are:
- The Law of Mentalism
- The Law of Correspondence
- The Law of Vibration

There are four Mutable Laws which means they are pliable can be transcended in ways that allow you to best work within them to create what is best for you and the reality you exist in. You can see why it would be very important to understand these laws. The universe doesn't conspire to hurt you, but ignorance of the Universal Laws can indeed do a great deal of harm in many unsuspecting ways.

The four Mutable Laws are:
- The Law of Polarity
- The Law of Rhythm
- The Law of Cause and Effect
- The Law of Gender

Some of this information comes from the *Metaphysical Dictionary* and some comes from the mystical teachings of the *Hermes Trismegistus* and the writings of the *kybalion*.

Back to the present!
The journey has taken me far, but today we seem to truly be back at the same place of our beginning, and are left with the same choice.
We find ourselves once again with the "The River Jordan Opportunity", where some will cross over and some will turn back.
It has always been your choice.
It is your choice, but to say it is a once in this lifetime decision doesn't accurately describe the importance of it. It is an extraordinary opportunity that only comes around once in a great age.

Chapter Eighteen

This changing world...

The world that my mother lived in doesn't exist anymore. The corruption of her generation was small compared to what we are experiencing today.

We live in a global world and in a global economy. Most of the politicians that are in power in Washington, D.C. have no real knowledge of what that means.

President Barack Obama knows, Bill and Hilary Clinton knows, George H and George W knows what living in a global world means, but the average Washington congressman elected in 2010 does not know, and that has continued to be a huge problem in the governing the United States in this global age.

Before we had a global economy, the United States aspired to be a land of high standards and enacted safeguards that kept America safe from pollution of air, water and minds. Our government knew that if it was left unchecked, and without government regulations, and oversight, it would open a path to ruin and the possibility irreparable damage.

As we moved into a global economy and our corporations began to recreate the old Wild, Wild West mentality of the emerging Eastern markets, they also discovered that there were no environmental protection agencies to content with; they discovered that there were no labor unions and no minimum wage laws to fight. In other words they realized they could produce their products without impunity in regards to human rights.

This gave them a sense of freedom from worry, if it hurt the environment, so what; if it was unfair for the workforce, so what. The end result was that businesses were free in the emerging markets to make their products without consequences to anything or anyone but the bottom line and the bottom line was profit. The lower the operating cost, the more profit that could be directed to the bottom line, the better the balance sheet looks, the higher the stocks rise, and the bigger the yearly bonus potential for those near the top. But for those at the top the reward was and is even greater.

There was no Social Security to pay into, no worker compensation to worry about, and no health insurance cost to be responsible for, but the best advantage was that with all the loop-holes that were voted into law over the years in the United States, meant there would be little or no taxes to pay. Remember the line "corporations are people too?" Now large corporations were reaping the harvest that their (loyal soldiers) congressman had sown.

The United States corporations became the bully in the boardroom with union leaders, and the bull in the china shop overseas, paving the way for polluting of pristine foreign lands and waters, while putting millions of people to work for a fraction of the cost of an American worker. While exacting concessions, they were at the same time moving those manufacturing jobs out of the United States; which removed the revenue stream from cities and towns thus were leaving the American worker, out of a job, out of hope, without any job replacement in sight.

Now we are left with the ramifications of the joblessness that has wrecked so many American manufacturing cities and towns across this country. The jobs are gone now; the intellectual property is also gone. Corporations told the American politician and the American worker not to be afraid of this change. They said we were moving into the information age and the American worker would be the keeper of the information and we would be the managers of the information. So far, this is not true, we are now twenty-seventh in education and are far behind, in four-year and beyond education. We are not manufacturing, we are not leading and we are not managing, so what is in store for us.

The things that would have made it true would have been advancements in science, math, biology and technology but alas we did not excel there either. The world is on schedule to catch and surpass us shortly, what will we do?

If you want intelligent minds you must fill them with intelligent thoughts, but we spent decades pouring none of that into the young minds that are our future. Instead, we have a society that has not imagined, has not created and has not built the things that will separate us in the world of the future and secure our place in the world.

If our youth's focus remains on reality shows, fifteen minutes of fame, texting, not talking, confining their words to 140 characters before they learn to build complicated and complex sentences we will forever be in trouble.

If, as a young person, you are allowed to feel that every meaningless thought uttered by you is important, it might lead to an inflated sense of self-worth, which may cause young people to want to cash in on their value long before they have done anything to merit it. With this grandiosity realized, they might start to think they are as important and as smart as anyone in the world and they might turn into people like the "Right Wing Talk Show" host, who think that there are only a few things wrong with America and that people in:

- Science
- Academia
- The entire Government

Should not be listened to because they are just wrong, there is no climate change, it is a hoax, people in academia are fools and the entire government is rigged. With a large segment of our society starting and thinking this way we are indeed in for a rough ride.

*Although, the bible offers a treasure trove of food for thought,
there are passages from other books that clarify, shape
and help refine your search.*

Chapter Nineteen

The Bible Augmented by Other Works

The bible talks about the battle for the Soul of the human-being, and the battle that takes place between good and evil. This battle in the bible rages on through the history of mankind, yet we are supposed to believe that life is so finite that it has only one beginning and one end. If this is true, and if we only have one chance to get it right, and if history is any example, we always get it wrong, then how does anyone ever get to live to tell the story? How does anyone survive the mistakes of the past to be a force in the future? How does information survive and revelations become revealed; and how do we as a society evolve more enlightened than before? The bible in its' literal interpretation does not tell us, nor is it supposed to tell us.

The original bible was the outline of the architect of creation and the formula for maintaining the universe. I am convinced that the original bible was written without obfuscation and hidden knowledge, I truly believe that came much later, maybe tens of thousands years later.

We are here by design, there are no accidents in the plan of God and there is so much more to us than merely the time and space we currently occupy.

I am of the belief that if you ask the question and seek the truth, the answer will come. Sometimes when it comes you may not always be ready for it. But, please do not throw it away, keep it, and put it on a shelf, until you are ready for it. It will be there and it will give you much needed information to help you with your quest when the time is right.

Over the year many books flowed to me as I continued to ponder the gaps in the bible and my inability to find the answers I sought, while as the same time, finding revelation after revelation in the bible, truly making it the most fascinating book on the planet.

As a book created for the layman, the general audience, it was not meant to reveal the secrets of the universe, yet each book and each verse had the potential to move the reader to ask a question and seek a higher meaning than was readily available in the passages given. It was this infusion of what was not there that repelled many a scholar to seek the higher meaning alluded to in the bible and guess what "seek and you will find, ask and it will be given unto you".

Yes the bible may not hand you the answers in bold print, but it does not mean that your answers will not be given. The bible can enables you to ask the right questions; the bible enables you to understand that there is more than what meets the eye; the bible can enables you to grow at your own pace, it does not cram information down your throat you are not yet able to swallow, it will allow you to digest small morsels of information at a time, to chew on, receive the nourishment from it, hunger for more and then search for more.

It really doesn't matter who decided to alter the bible, to tailor its contents to suit the church of the day. It simply doesn't matter, the bible lives to serve man where man's intellect and spirituality is at any given moment in time. The saying from the movie A Few Good Men, "you can't handle the truth" is true at some point in time in all our lives. As we grow and accumulate knowledge, understanding and hopefully wisdom we are able to grasp more and more about the human spirit and its place in the larger universe. When we get to that place in our evolutionary journey, more is revealed and the journey into higher learning continues throughout the rest of our lives.

As more and more is revealed, our yearning to know more is so inherit in our nature, we cannot turn back, our yearning to know God and all the wonders of the universe causes us to continue to seek and expand our thinking.

The prayer of Jabez is one of those hidden meaning passages in the bible. It is perfect in its literal meaning, but it is also perfect in its esoteric more complex meaning. Please God, expand the territory of my mind and enrich my knowledge. It is a powerful request, and just as Jabez has the audacity to ask God to do so, so do we, but to do so, first, it must mean that you know, and believe in the power of God to do so, and also in your ability and right to ask. It takes a lot of knowledge and understanding of the language of the bible to get to this point in your evolutionary journey and it may take you many trips through the Psalms to get there.

The twenty-third Psalm will get you there the minute you believe it with your whole being. It is truly a powerful knowing and a powerful awakening. It places your trust in God as the focus of your health and well-being under any and all circumstances. It takes fear of the unknown out of the equations and it puts you on a path to outpace all of your enemies because they are all afraid of something that you do not have to fear.

I must confess that I did not get all of my revelations from just reading the bible, but the bible is the only book I spent decades reading and re-reading and using as research. It is the only source I use to back up other books that portray themselves as the truth and the way. Other books are gap fillers, the truth is already there. There are many books that help fill in the gaps, and expand the conversation into the mysteries written about in the bible.

The Aquarian Gospel of Jesus The Christ was one of the early books that came to me to ponder and it made me a happy follower of The Christ teaching. It put the way one should live in relationship to the rest of the human-kind in prospective. We are our brothers and sisters keepers, we are one, what is done to one is truly done to all. When we start to live as if what we think and what we do affects everything and everyone, not just ourselves, we start to live responsibly. It was the right book at the right moment to cement the foundation the bible laid for me.

I was visiting my best friend for the weekend, when I first saw this book. I had gotten up early and found it on a reading table. The title caught my attention, so I curled up in a comfortable and started reading. I fell in love, with God's love that morning, it opened a new understanding of the true meaning of how a loving God operates and expresses love.

The *Celestine Prophecy* series was another set of books that helped to expand my thinking and enlarge my territory as additional knowledge continued to flow through the books I was privileged to come across. The Celestine Prophecy was about living in the moment and being totally aware of what you are trying to tell yourself. The body is full of information, but as we multitask, and let other things occupy our thoughts and take our energy, we are not aware that the opportunity to expand our mind, our consciousness have passed and we have lost yet another opportunity to be one with the universe and one with God. We lose the opportunity to be in tune with God and sadly instead we remained out of sync.

The book further helped me to train my mind to control, anger and frustration and realize that all energy is living and that the energy we give off has the ability to change everything around us. In other words, if I am angry, that anger is projected on to everything around me and changes every situation for the worse, while if I am calm and emote love even in stressful situations, all around me would receive the positive energy I put out, and love would be enough to change any situation to the best outcome the moment would allow.

Although, not every outcome would have the desired outcome, it would never be as bad as its opposite reaction.

The Secret Doctrine came at a time when I was seeking to unlock the secrets of the universe and this book helped me to understand that the history of the universe included more than just our world. It helped me to understand that the bible had not made a mistake when it said heavens as a plural. The expanse of the realm of God was so vast that we would not be able in any circumstance to comprehend how life evolved beyond our known planet or how the world might interact with one another.

The *Sirius Mysteries* was a book recommended to me at a social gathering, I had never heard of it but was really interested in reading it. At the next gathering, the book was presented to me with this quote, "this book was meant for you to have." I am so grateful to have received such an important book on my journey. The book clearly outlined how the star Sirius A and B is related to planet Earth and was known to America through an African Tribe called the *Dogon Tribe* who documented the planet existence some five thousand years ago, long before any telescope could see the existence of the small Sirius B star.

But it was The *Urantia Book* that brought it all home for me. This book filled in the one gap that no other book had ever broached. It expanded the golden cord and the soul, the reason why the cord is cut, the discontinuance of life and the continuance of life.

It explains the use the terminology used in the bible of those who were set-a-side, chosen, elect, it let us understand why the division came about and why and it explains the one burning question I had.

Because of its explanation I am now convinced more than ever that the master plan of the Universal God will always win out. The garden will be cultivated down through the ages, and what is planted will have the sun and the rain needed to insure that the good seeds are nourished and nurtured and that their territories are enlarged and enriched.

According to *Urantia* it is the personality (soul) that can survive throughout eternity. It doesn't matter what you physically look like; it doesn't matter where you live; it doesn't matter whether you are well-off or barely making it. What does matter is where your heart is and if it is aligned with God as your center. If God is at your center than all of your decision-making will reflect who is at the center of your life. People will know who you are, without you ever having to tell them. Your actions will speak louder than any words you could possibility utter. Where you place your energies and what you hope for, will tell a better story about yourself than any description of yourself you could give.

Have you tried to make the world a better place throughout your life, or have you tried to make yourself better without regard for the world around you? Have you lived a life that can be recognized by your character?

The Urantia Book reinforces the bible's hidden information and brings light to questions that before had no answers. But I will fully admit it also contains some things I am not in agreement with, which is my choice. Some things in the book I found no shelf space for, so I readily let them fall away, as it should be with anything that doesn't resonate with your spirit.

The ways of the people of pre-history are spoken of in the beautiful "Odes of Solomon" which was taken out of the bible.

Narrative taken from *The Lost Books of the Bible and the Forgotten Book of Eden*

"Here are some of the most beautiful songs of peace and joy that the world possesses. Yet their origin, the date of their writing, and the exact meaning of many of the verses remain on the great literary mysteries.
They have come down to us in a single and very ancient document in Syriac language. Evidently that document is a translation from the original Greek. Critical debate has raged around these Odes; one of the most plausible explanations is that they are songs of newly baptized Christians of the First Century.
They are strangely lacking in historical allusions. Their radiance is no reflection of other days. They do not borrow from either the Old Testament or the Gospels. The inspiration of these verses is first-hand. The remind you of Aristides' remark, "A new people with whom something Divine is mingled." Here is vigor and insight to which we can find parallels only in the most exalted parts of the Scriptures."

For these dazzling mystery odes, we owe our translation to J. Rendel Harris, M.A., Hon, Fellow of Clare College, Cambridge. He says about them: *"There does not seem to be anything about which everyone seems to agree unless it be that the Odes are of singular beauty and high spiritual value."*
Excerpts taken from The Lost Books of the Bible and the forgotten books of Eden
World Bible Publishers, Inc 1926 by Alpha House

"The assumptions that J. Rendel Harris makes are:

1. *Is that you cannot determine when the Odes were written, because he was already predisposed to exclude anything perceived as pre-history*
2. *That the Syriac document had to have been translated from the Greek, which although a part of his education to believe that the Greek were the first translators of all there is, was wrong. The Syriac document was probably translated from the original cuneiform tablet*
3. *That the Odes must be from the first century Christian era, instead of the original worship of the trinity which started with Osiris, Isis and Horus*
4. *He would just have to discount the facts of a total lack of continuity between the Odes and all other written work. They don't read like the Old Testament or the Gospels*
5. *He also had to discount Aristides' remark, "A new people with whom something Divine is mingled." And admission that people of divine character did exist in that time and space*

6.   *The Odes while everyone agreed were a singular beauty and of high spiritual vale were not included in the bible. You have to ask yourself, why? Could it be that the essence of the Son of Man was in the world before the Christian era and there were people on earth that believed and loved peace and all God's creatures. People who were also followers of the great teacher in pre-history times"*

In the introduction to the second book in the Lost Book, the Forgotten Books of Eden I found the following passages that I think are of great interest and shed insight.

"An American Indian's Song is his very own. No other man can sing it without his explicit permission....

To sing another's song is an invasion of this personality, a sort of spiritual piracy involving sacrilege."

Also this one...

"Indeed, by the Hebrews a story was popularly presumed to have its hero for its author......

So for centuries among the Jews, writers sought to shelter themselves behind the names of the great dead. In this way they were guilty of no fraud."

I have always been on a search to answers to questions I had had for a long time. I think there are many people that have also had the same questions and I think that there are some that know the answers, but have not revealed the answers to the general populace. Which means, for me, that they have revealed them to some group or some entity, and this of course, leads to other questions, the biggest ones are why, and to whom? Why not tell this amazing finding, why not inform those who have a need to know, why not make contact with all the interested parties, why not share, what could the reason possibly be to not do so?

- What does it could it change?
- What does it do to the history of the universe?
- Would it change the balance of power in the world?
- Would it change the make-up of the world's power structure?
- Will it change anything?
- Will it make people view God differently?
- Will it make people look at their religion differently?
- Will it change our destiny?
- Is there some group out there that thinks letting this information out of the bag it a game changer?
- Will the old game be in jeopardy?
- Will the balance of power shift?

Maybe, just maybe, I really hadn't thought about that, but maybe that is the answer.

There are moments of clarity in the bible that led me to continue my research from a biblical perspective. So many theologians tell us to look at the bible as a literal read and to take it on its face value. This is all well and good when you are a child, but when you grow up, you really need to put away childish things and childish explanations.

When a person enters seminary they are exposed to some hidden meanings in the bible's chapters and verses. Yes, the bible is a literal read, but it is also chopped full of other meanings for those who need to know. As your need to know increases with your level of knowledge and respect for what you have learned, the mysteries of the bible continue to unfold and other complimentary works will also come into your consciousness to help you with your studies, as it did with me.

There are so many sciences in the bible that we never talk about, why, I would like to ask? Science is a part of our lives, we would not be alive to without science, yet we are stopped from talking about it from a biblical standpoint, why? It was featured prominently in the books that were left out of the bible. I read those books as well and found that while they went into greater detail, their essence was not entirely left out of the bible. So on top of the hidden mysteries in the bible, there were also the hidden mysteries left out of the bible.

Time and time again!

Chapter Twenty

Three Talked about Periods in Known History

I have discovered that there are at least three periods in history that need to be understood, in order to begin to put the history of our known world in context.

The first period which we know very little about is the time called "In the beginning." It includes the creation of the planet earth and it is also the time that includes the period of humankind's access to both the heavenly realm, and the newly formed earthly realm.

The second period chronicles the early life and times on earth in search of God and the understanding of God through the creation of little gods.

The third period is the period where the old ways give way to the belief in one God and ultimately the need and acceptance of one savior.

The truth though is that this all happened in a time that is now called pre-history, and pre-history, has all but been deleted from today's history. It is glossed over by historians and reframers of history. By drawing a line in time and space and calling it all "pre-history" it allowed them to rewrite the true history into a different time and space and give it to a completely different group of people to legitimize their claim as the chosen people of the bible as the inheritors of all that God had bestowed upon the original "chosen".

The truth was never uncovered completely enough to get attention from a mainstream audience outside of the highest academic circles. The books on college shelves were carefully chosen not to include any books that would refute for the discerning individual the usurpation of the original history or the knowledge of the original people.

The audacity of calling the people of God pre-history is a very telling statement. It actually is saying that the heavenly realm of God has no place in our interpretation of history and no place in our society. I know that this is a terrible statement to make, but I intend to prove that this statement has validity in context with the history of the period of time and space that was reinterpreted.

To understand that there were two groups of people on the land, occupying it at different times, instead of at the same time, that shaped the world we know today, but only one was given credit for everything, which I now know was not true and is worth proving.

The first place that led me to believe that something was missing was as I said before the bible, but the missing books of the bible offered some great insight as to why they were excluded, and why they were important to the true history of God and man.

When we look at the world today, and see that so many, God fearing Christians, call for hurtful things to be done to the rest of the human race without regard to life, liberty, or the pursuit of happiness; you start to wonder how God fearing Christians could act this way. Then all you have to do is go to the bible and witness all of the hate, killing, war and mayhem in the name of God's people to see the prototype for today mayhem is still playing out. You may ask yourself, why would God create such a people to run such a world and hurt so many people in His name? The simple truth is, He wouldn't but man would. By taking the so called pre-history, history out of today's bible, God's original people and their ways were not privy to people wanting to know that there was a better way to live that God had in mind. They would have found out that "created in our image" meant with love and light, not darkness, hate and greed.

Did you notice here that the mingling of two distinct people in one text, we start out with the original Hebrew writers of the biblical text and that a few paragraphs later by coupling everything before mentioned to the Jewish people, which were two different sects of people in two different periods of time and space. In the Pre-history days of which we know nothing, that we can record as history, there certainly was not a Jewish race of people. There was however people on the earth, because it was recorded in Genesis in the first earth age. They were the people of the first Adam and Eve, the people of the first Eden.

These people were the called the "originals" by a few historians blessed to see beyond the veil of secrecy and into the world of a privileged few. The "originals" were written about in the bible in very unique ways that manage to seep into the narrative in ways that did not disturb the blanket of secrecy perpetrated on an unsuspecting reader.

Since the Hebrew people existed during the first earth age and the Jewish people existed after the first earth age, they cannot be intermingled, interchanged, or blended to shrink history into one neat little package, to make a small portion of the world's population be masters of the human race of billions of other people unlike themselves.

"The figure of the Messiah which Jesus adapted to his creative purpose cannot be imagined by a modern without a perusal of the book of Enoch which is its classic and most entrancing glorification. Without the Odes and Songs of Solomon the atmosphere breathed by the earliest church cannot be divined.
Hitherto access to this literature has been confined to technical scholars. Its assembly would require special information and considerable expenditure. With this enterprise of the Alpha House, Inc., it becomes democratic property. We shall have a more intelligent clergy and laity, when this volume has taken its place in every library, and is familiarly brought into every discussion of the historic Christ and His times." The Lost Books of the Bible

The most important thing about this passage is that the reader found the language to be strikingly different and in harmony with something outside of the known religious orders of today. The Odes and Songs of Solomon and the atmosphere cannot be recreated today. It is just that different.

I will continue to bring you evidence of the "originals" for their story is buried in pre-history and obfuscated as it was brought forth in our current history as the history of a more modern time and space. The truth is unfolding though, and we will unseal the many books and passages for a new look at an old text for new and revealing insight.

Prelude to a new day
The end and the beginning is upon us

A movie starts ending, the moment it begins.
Our lives start ending, the moment we are born.
This earth age started ending, the moment it began.
we are almost at that point again...
Look for the signs and wonders
11-11-11
12-12-12
13-13-13
144,000

Chapter Twenty-One

Some Things Must End,
So New Things can Begin

Of course, it has been ending since it began. But now that we are, in my opinion, nearing the end of the cycle, and judging by the unfolding events, that have occurred since the close of 12-12-12 or the end of the Hopi Calendar, a change is certainly a feasible assumption.

Once again we can look to the bible for references of the times in which we find ourselves:

- Matthew 24:24 speaks of false christs and false prophets
- Mark 16:16-17, shows that there is a distinct difference in the destination of souls even if salvation is misleading the need for it is apparent.
- 2nd Timothy 3:15, perilous times shall come in the last days.
- 1 Thessalonians 5:3, liking the times to come as feeling like a woman in labor, the labor does not stop until the baby is birthed.
- Revelation 12:1, the appearance of the great wonder in heaven; a woman clothed with the sun, the moon under her feet and upon her head a crown of twelve stars.

It is this verse in Revelation that needs particular attention. It is this passage that has never been fully explained or taught to me in any bible study session I have ever attended. I personally thank the glorious *Thoughtland* for clarity.

Look closely:

- A great wonder in heaven – yes!
- A woman – yes!
- With the sun and the moon under <u>her</u> feet – yes!
- We see the sun and the moon every day as we look up – yes!
- A crown of twelve stars on her head – yes!

This represents the infinite space beyond our reach of astronomy and astrology and it heralds the return of the Feminine energy into our atmosphere at a time when it is needed most. But the entrance will also bring consequences and necessary corrections.

The Return of the 144,000…

The return of the 144,000 represents a time of completion; a unit of divine world (a unit of God) 4 of the 10(the perfect cube); the number of cubits that measures the ramparts of Celestial Jerusalem in Revelation 21:17
Revelation 7, sites the four angels located in the four corners of the world, which I have determined for myself are the sealed children of the light, who were indeed sealed before the foundation of the earth. Note sealed and saved are not now nor have ever been known to be the same thing. It has been a misleading statement and assumption fostered down through the ages and firmly established in today's scholarly rhetoric and writings.
The 144,000 number is of major importance and is paramount to the foundation and premise of this book. What would it serve to uncover the children of the light, if their identification was all that we needed to know? No person or group is sealed, and the very title is so coveted, without good reason.
The 144,000 or the Children of the Light are essential to the return of the Divine Source. They are the Calvary, they have been preserved for just such a moment, to help usher in a new dispensation period.
The Bible and the biblical works included or not speak of the *Lost Tribe of Israel*, which although while telling the story in literal terms is still speaking of the Children of Light, as they were indeed lost to the consciousness of the world.
In Daniel 9:24-27, the 144,000 were called the first fruits, God's own, Her beloved. It can't get any plainer than that, can it?
In Ephesians 1:13-14, the inheritance promised to us in Christ and sealed by the Holy Spirit. Co-heirs with Christ in Romans 8:17. Co-heirs would means having the same attributes, rights and privileges of the Christ.
The bible acknowledges that there are those who are like the iconic Christ including the inheritance of everlasting life, that even if they die a physical death, they will rise in Trinity time (a figurative three days).
Since we do not know how many human existed before the exodus from heaven, we have no way of ever knowing what the actual number of the sealed represent which is why it is cubed. It is infinite in nature and feared by any that would not benefit from such a return or collective gathering.
At the end of the cycle of 12-12-12, the Hopi sages could see no further. It was the end of the governmental cycle of the age, and the entrance into the 13th cycle. It was the end and the beginning.

It heralded the end of the masculine energy dominance that ruled with absolute power over the earthly realm and the return of the feminine energy.

It heralded the end of the turbulence that gripped the world and the beginning of a new harmonious love vibration that will awake every child of light and child of God.

The twelve signs of the Zodiac all have their place in the universe and are among the signs and wonders we are able to look to for discernment.

The Thirteenth tribe references…

The bible and the historians conveniently separate the twelve tribes from the thirteenth tribe, so that we never think that there were ever any more than just the twelve. The thirteenth is mentioned as different; as lost; as not legitimate somehow. This of course makes it of great interest to me for several reasons.

A chart of the priesthood itself reveals that a branch of the Levitical priesthood the Merari was under Jacob, and as I recall the true Jacob Ladder took place when there was indeed a divine connection between heaven and earth through the Jacob's ladder. If the Merari of the Levitical priesthood was in Jacob that would make it a part of the heavenly priesthood is well.

It is said that Seventy (70) of the Merari priests went with Joseph down into Egypt which is very interesting don't you think. There could be another way of say "Lost." We also know that the number 70 is a spiritually complete number that is used symbolically to denote a higher meaning.

I have also learned that Egypt is used in the bible not as a physical place but as a representation of opulence grandeur and everything other worldly and set apart, and made it the enemy of all living on the earth. As if the war was with Egypt, and not one's self.

If this is true and I suspect it is, what does Egypt really represent? Could Egypt be the remnants of the grandeur that existed when heaven and earth were indeed not separated, but were connected by Jacob's ladder and the divine priesthood of Meari, the original Levi Priesthood, who would have reported directly to Melchizedek, high priest forever?

The thirteenth tribe of Israel was mentioned with the number 70 connected to it. Seventy is not just a literal number, it is also a symbolic number and therefore it is quite possible that the Lost Tribe of Israel, that went down in Egypt actually returned to the heavenly realm before the metaphoric portal, gateway, bridge, river was closed.

Since the thirteenth tribe was always set aside as the tribe of the royal priesthood, it would make sense that they would follow Joseph as he went down to Egypt.

This leads to the answer of why the Aaron Priesthood really needed to be established.

The entrance of the thirteenth Zodiac, which, since each zodiac sign represents a different tribe of Israel, so the lost tribe of Israel is not represented as well.

The appearance of the thirteenth zodiac sign Ophiuchus which is visible today and has been since August 21, 2013 and has been perceived differently depending which camp you sit in.
The attributes of Ophiuchus are:
- Healer
- Able to bring the dead back to life (an attribute of the Christ)
- Also known as Serpentarius the Serpent Holder which was depicted as a man holding a snake which he divided in half and is also known as Enki a Sumerian god.

The new Zodiac line-up put Ophiuchus between Scorpio and Sagittarius which gives credence to the fact that indeed new energy has entered into our atmosphere which is disconcerting to many folks.

Thinking of it in strictly layman's terms how I reacted to the universe before is not how I am reacting now. Things may be affecting you differently; you may seem to want different things; your body may seem to need different things, and you may want to scream and holler, but change is coming in you and through you. It is a good thing. Embrace the new you that is emerging, and celebrate that you have been chosen to change for the better.

If you feel peace and calmness, if the outside world seems like a bad movie you are watching, you are also in good company for there are many on all sides of this equation of coming into the next phase of our eternal existence. But we have much work to do.

The Coming Tribulation Period…

The tribulation period spoken of in the bible had a certain amount of time associated with it, but we have ascertained that time is an earthy construct and has no value in the mind of the Most High God.

But what I will say that all the signs are pointing to us being in the biblical tribulation period, and if so, we will be in it however long it will last. This knowledge alone should be a wake-up call for those who still think they have time to get it back later. Now is now!

We have certainly seen the rise of false prophets in all genres of society from the political, financial and the pulpit.

At the end of the Hopi Calendar and the end of the gestation period, and the end of a spiritual time comes a time of reckoning. We are in such a time.

The world right now is full of chaos and turmoil. This time we are in will continue as it reacts to the new cleansing energies, that will increasingly enter into the atmosphere.

The new energies are not compatible with every person on the face of the earth. But the new energies will allow the masks that people wear to fall away. It will also allow the scales of blindness to fall away and will give all persons the ability to see clearly and to hear clearly. And they who have ears to hear and eyes to see, the Most High God will be shown to them.

The 13th Aeon is just below the Source of Light and the Region of the Mist. The other side is through the mist, which is where great faith comes in, for in 2nd Corinthians 5:7 it states, "We walk by faith, not by sight."

The return of the Thirteenth in bible speak is recording as the Lost Tribe, the Tribe of Levi was recorded in the bible as the first acknowledgement of a thirteenth tribe. The Tribe of Levi was set apart, they were different, they were unique and they were the keepers of the religious worship centers. Was it because they had knowledge of the way home? Was it because they held a certain power?

The time of the return of the Divine Mother which will indeed usher in the dispensation filled with feminine energy of love, mercy, compassion, justice, and generosity which will rain down on the planet and the cleanse the soil of the blood from the vinepresses.

The Dye is cast and sealed for:
11-11-11
12-12-12
13-13-13
144,000

Chapter Twenty-Two

Symbolic Numbers

The numbers you find that have great meaning in the bible will jump out at you once you fully realize just how very significant they are to the telling of the story of hidden things.

The numbers 2, 3, 7, 9, 12, 33, 144,000 and the combinations of 11-11, 12-12, and 13-13 conspicuously left out of the conversation all together. Didn't you just want to know why that particular number was just about vanished from our lexicon?

The bible places great emphasis on these numbers to explain things beyond our lay understanding, and leaves it up to the interpretation of others who may or may not have the necessary foundation or discernment to explain them correctly. But each thing that jumps out at you has significance to you for you, and about you and your evolutionary path. Remember this when you desire to grow and to know how to grow, the universe will conspire to help you in every way possible, by using every resource available.

Sacred Geometry is practiced in the bible as enlightenment for the learned, the scholarly and the seeker.
"Seek and you shall find; knock and the door will be opened". This crumb was left there for you to find.

Sacred Geometry is a key to any attempt of understanding the Universal Mind. It is a noble attempt, one that will never be fully known because it is the Unknowable, but one that can bear fruit for our evolutionary growth, as it was intended to do.

Sacred Geometry insists in everything, nothing escapes it for everything was created out of it and is maintained through it.

The patterns and symbolic codes offer wisdom and knowledge that we can use for the betterment of self and humankind. If only we collectively knew this and how to use it, only the Most High God knows how far we would have already traveled on the spiral upward toward Her presence.

But here we are without the collective power that sacred geometry would have brought; here we stand without the knowledge that within the sacred geometry lies the diversity of all things and the uniqueness of all things, that when working together create everything throughout everything, even us. We are all connected and we all experience fear, anger, hurt, sorrow and joy for within sacred geometry is the knowledge that it is all controlled by the energy of the universe.

The equations for Pi, The Square Root of Two, and The Golden Ratio equate irrational numbers, and their presence, which you will find everywhere are still unable to be fully comprehended on this planet. If the dark could fully understand their sacred meanings, I do not believe this world would still be in existence.

We are held together by the Golden Ratio which some Gnostics call the Golden Cord. I had never put this two and two together before. But when you look at the simplest explanation for the Golden Ratio is that it is the unique ratio that links us to the continuity of all relationships from our beginning.

The Chinese Book of Changes speaks of the Yin and Yang lines and the water they are immersed in. Yet we are not taught what any of this means, it is a college elective course or part of a major or minor in Asian or Chinese studies. Yet, it is not for the average persons' knowledge bank. But the very fact that it also includes the conversation about the Judgment, the Abysmal and the separation of the lower realms from the upper realm which I think are separated by the 13th region of the heavens, makes it important for all to study and to know.

The number three is referenced there, its' significance is inescapable through time and space it has shown up in every culture as an important number. We cannot ignore the signs and wonders; they are the guides we ask for even when we don't recognize them when they show up.

Just as this small knowing, that numbers are able to be calculated and bring meaning to our lives, is taboo, in many mainstream Western societies, and in the bible although the same bible uses them extensively.

How can both be true, that it is bad and good at the same time to use numbers which is a simple version of sacred geometry?

It is used by astrologers, astronomers, scientists and mathematicians alike because they know that in order to do their jobs, these were the necessary tools they need to use, to get from point A to point B.

We ordinary Western tradition folks do not know this and therefore charting our course is much harder without all the advantages of knowing sacred geometry many uses.

I can't help you to understand its inner working, but I can help you to be aware that you should look into it for yourself. Look and you shall find. Seek and it shall be given. Those in the dark are searching, but they will never see the light, and without the light, they will search in vain, but you, my friend, are cut from a different cloth, and can glean exactly what is meant for you, because the LIGHT is in you and your greatest benefactor.

For those that have ears to hear this verse is very important.
Revelation 17:1-18
and there came one of the seven angels which had the seven vials, and talked with me, saying unto me, come hither; I will shew unto thee the judgement of the great whore that sitteth upon many waters.

I read this many times or heard it read many times and never once thought it was possibly a reference to the Divine Mother, but sadly my eyes see clearly now and I hear with different ears.

What man would write such a thing about the Great Mother, who would blaspheme in such a way? I can only think of those who had not received the divine inheritance and knew what it meant to have not received it or earned it. It could only be those who understood what the loss of divine privileges could do to one's existence. It could only come from those who felt the fear of losing what little power they had on the earthly realm, which although is nothing compared to the heavenly realm, but it is all they have and the coming tribulation period is a definite threat to their kingdom. But I now say blaspheme away it won't change the outcome, some laws are immutable.

The Unveiling of Those of Unknown Origin is Coming Soon

Throughout history they (the almighty great ones) have told us about the impending doom that would determine our future and very earthly existence.

They have warned us that we would have to take sides and take a stand and could no longer be fence sitter has the war raged around us, as did the biblical seven churches that Paul visited.

History books, obscure out of print ancient books and modern literature all point to a time of great warfare and reckoning; a time when decisions have to be made about which side of the equation each individual will stand.

It also points to a group of people predestined to work for the good of all. They will come forth and stand with the Right at this historic time.

The bible calls these people the "chosen". Although groups have calmed this title throughout history, the actual purpose of this group has a specific time period in which to come forth. They appearance will be determined by the advent of the second coming, which negates any other so called "chosen". The real 'chosen" have lead doormat and unknown to us and themselves throughout history. No one knows who they are or why they really exist or that they exist, how they will be identified and called into service and least of all what they can do to assist in a change in the course of history.

Mythology has claimed them; the bible has called them the 144,000 who will fight the Anti-Christ; but no one knows how or when they will be called or how they will respond or how they will be identified and if no one knows who they are then how would they know themselves?

The history books tell us about the heroic few that will rise up to save the many. The bible is full of these tales of valor, small men defeating giants, small armies defeated very larger armies, small villages standing against the mighty King's army. There is no lack of examples of what a few can do when "right" is on their side, as recorded throughout the annuls of history.
It cannot be by chance, because the design of the universes and its inhabitants are too intricate a design for anything like this to be left to chance.

So, then the question is, what was done, in the beginning, to ensure their safety and to obfuscate this chosen group?

The bible talks openly about the chosen; the elect; the set-aside; without ever letting you know how they will be identified in modern times.

Science fiction talks openly about the battle to expose those who fight against all manners of darkness. The running themes in the ancient texts, mythology and into the modern era, is the war that the bible calls the battle for the souls of men.

Great civilizations have come and gone, rising to greatness only to succumb to the temptations of darkness. Each new civilization having the opportunity to be better than its predecessor eventually fell short of their desired goal.

Each civilization having the ability to make a better world, to create a responsible society, that would leave a stronger foundation than they started with, and one that would benefit all of humanity, and nurture the earth, chose not to do so. Time and time again people were sacrificed for material gain, be it power, prestige, resources or slaves. In the end, neither land nor people benefited.

Power in each civilization superseded the humane and earthy good making it hard to build a world and a people not destined to be destroyed.

The old world was so entrenched in war that a new world was sort and the brave new world was found in the Western Hemisphere, and they called it America.

People of all persuasions flocked to the new world to escape the tyranny of the lands they left.

The new world brought new hopes and dreams that finally there would be a beckon of light in a world of darkness, and that this new world would be an opportunity to change the course of history for good.

Religious freedom seekers came; equality in the arts seeking enthusiasts came; people wanting to have a chance at a fresh start after a bad run came; and with them came those that wanted to get rich and saw this the opportunity of a lifetime; they all came and they all had the opportunity to make this brave new world the greatest place on earth.

But the people of the different tribes of North America were in their way and had to be removed or pushed aside. Then there was the fact that the land could be a stubborn step-child and hard to manage for them alone and they needed help. It was just too hard for them, so the slave ships starred to arrive and didn't stop for centuries.

The seeds of the new world were sown in blood, and the fruits were filled with a bitterness, that would come out in the elite as sour grapes and even the sweetest sugar could not change. It seems that old habits die hard if they die at all. The tenets of the old world had made its way into the new world and into the governing laws of the land and in many ways became far worse than anything previously known.

So this new landscape of earth was inhabited and governed, but to the universal watchers, the gods or the Elohim, it was not a time to celebrate for the results were not the outcomes the desired outcomes, nor would they be in the future, of this they were sure.

They always knew that if there was no worthy turnaround, there would have to be a divine intervention, as was spoken of throughout history in both ancient and modern text.

But, who would it be? Comic books suggest a hero and/or bands of hero's with great and mighty powers that will fight great battles against Aliens or evil-doers always winning and saving the world.

The bible talks of the second coming in which a war would be fought in the air. This is an interesting scenario because if you look deep into its meaning, it seems to suggest spiritual not physical warfare.

If you ask and I hope you do, what is the difference between spiritual and physical warfare? I will tell you, it is big. Physical warfare we are used to and even if you don't see the first punch coming, you know you are in a fight when the blow lands. But with spiritual warfare, it is different. You may get worn down without ever knowing you are in a battle. There is a reason we surround ourselves with the Light and Love of Jesus the Christ or the Blue White Light of the Most High God. It is because we are seeking the hedge of protection from spiritual warfare. What we may not recognize is that the enemy uses things that we deem innocent and therefore we let our guard down or even worse we never put it up.

We can become bombarded with warfare from sources we are not aware of or much less prepared to fight. The difference is great, so great, that if you do not see it physically you may miss its coming and lose the war before you get a chance to fight it.

With the advent of the rapidly changing technology world, new technology is available and being used, long before the average person is aware it has even left the drawing board. Most medical and technology trails to prove theories are now being tested by the public without their knowledge or approval, with only the initial testing is done in labs. The results are tabulated and decisions are made based not on the efficacy of the test results of the technology product, but on the go to market important profit-margin.

If the profit outweighs the risk to the public the product will be given the green light and unleashed on an unsuspecting public. Some of this new technology may work on you at the spiritual level. This is frighteningly true.

Return of the Divine Mother!
Re-entry of Feminine Energy!
Coming Grace!
Acceptance!
Forgiveness!
Salvation!
Oneness!

Chapter Twenty-Three

Return of the Divine Mother

The Seven Churches

T he story of the Seven Churches in the Book of Revelation is
something I grew up hearing about in church, over and over again. Our
congregations always thought it was talking to the church, and we would
try to figure out which one our own church most identified with, but right
there in Revelation chapter 1 we have completely ignored what it actually
said.
*"The Revelation of Jesus Christ, which God gave unto him, to shew unto his
servants things which must shortly come to pass; and he sent and signified it by
his angel unto his servant John:*
*2 Who bare record of the word of God, and of the testimony of Jesus Christ, and of
all things that he saw.*
*3 Blessed is he that readeth, and they that hear the words of this prophecy, and keep
those things which are written therein: for the time is at hand."*
     The coded symbolism of the bible speaks about the end of the
Dispensation in the parable of the Seven Churches, which although
separated in the bible is directly related to the opening of the Seven Seals.
     What is not told in the bible is how it all individually relates to us
in our daily lives and in our spiritual and physical lives.
"Everything we will ever need is here now."
     This phrase is repeated by the Gnostics throughout time. I always
thought that this has to mean something. I now know it is related to our
inherit ability to effect change within our own environment, in our own
small universe.
     When we look at the Seven Churches in relationship to ourselves
and how the human body infuses and stores energy, then we can begin to
understand the parable better.
     The one thing that was hard for me to grasp, as a novice in these
matters, was exactly how the Seven Churches related to me as an
individual. Yet, as I sat in sermons or lectures, the difference between
brick and mortar, flesh and blood, and my ability to effect change could
not be reconciled in my brain.

The reason for my brain's confusion was because a valuable knowing was not yet known and had not been taught to me at that time.

If it had been, I would have been able to see our relationship to everything and known about our individual responsibility and ability to effect positive change.

With forthright information of the interrelationship of the parable about our opportunity for personal growth, which could lead to our upward spiral, the parable of the Seven Churches, as presented, had no showing of good faith to the faithful.

As it turns out, the churches, in the mind of the Most High God and the Christ were never brick and mortar but in "we the people".

Remember when Jesus was twelve (meaning he had reached the governmental completion cycle) and he went to the temple to speak to the priests... or remember when he went to the temple and turned over the table of the tax collector? He was not a fan of brick and mortar, and his greatest moments were not to large congregations of church leaders in their temples for he had great disdain for them. He preferred a hillside where anyone could gather and hear his message and share some food.

The fact that the bible clearly puts him at twelve years old, which means governmental completeness, probably means that this period of time as referenced in the bible was the beginning of another dispensation period. Remember, how I told you everything written, has sort of been amalgamated together, and presents a very incoherent literal story? This is a great example of what I began to see.

The fact that his teachings were later taken over by the church and stripped of their original meaning and boiled down to a few sound bites, is a wrong that should be made right.
In the early years of the twenty first century maybe two thousand one or two, I did a lecture on the Seven Churches, as a new and powerful knowing that had just come into my consciousness.

Although, it is hard to change the body politic of the church and its culture, we can change ourselves and leave food for thought for others.

Religion did not start in the West, yet when the West took spirituality out of religion and proceeded to make everything about brick and mortar, it was at this point in time when religion became about worldly possessions, and when all meanings in the bible started to come from a more physical slant, rather than a spiritual point of view. This curtailed or greatly reduced any chances we had for spiritual enlightenment ever coming from the brick and mortar establishments, and for those most in need of it.

Why was the true knowledge of the Seven Churches separated from the people?

In my opinion, it was separated because the Seven Churches of the bible is a metaphor for the Seven Chakras of the human body. The human body, don't we all want to know what the Most High God had to say about our body's relationship to the Seven Churches, doesn't this seem important? The good news is that every church could and should be teaching this information, but the bad is it apparently is not.

The truth is, each of the seven churches represents a different body chakra, and all chakras are connected for the successful flow of energy from the bottom to the top. The growth of the individual is determined by how well the energy is able to spiral upward through the spinal column.

Each church represents the obstacles the individual encounters and must overcome on their journey upward and homeward.

The energy flow can get stalled anywhere along the way as there are a myriad of reasons that progress can slowdown or cease to freely move upward.

The churches have descriptive reasons, but since the reasons given were designed to buy into the church's current indoctrination, it wasn't a recipe for your growth and salvation. It was a recipe for the church's growth and salvation which continuously uses you as its savior and its provider.

What are chakras?

Chakra is a Sanskrit word which means wheels or vortex as it refers to the seven energy centers of which, our consciousness and our energy center is composed. It is the system of the body in which energy is transferred, as if it were a train running on a track, with on and off switches and red and green lights, as well as full throttle ahead action filled with the endless possibilities one can obtain.

While the chakra system may be on the mainline, there are thousands of small lines that feed into, and are fed by the chakra system, all of which we, in the Western world know very little, but are well known and quite commonly spoken about in the Eastern world.

Our spiritual, physical, and biological functions are all tied up in the inner workings of the chakra system, and we have an invested interest in the outcome of a properly functioning chakra system. Yet there is no traditional Western church to help us, and there is no mainstream doctor to educate us, on the true workings and needs of the human body for our evolutionary growth and wellness.

This is the current sad state of how western medicine is controlled, yet again, by brick and mortar, and not by a desire to save anyone but it. I am not saying anything to disparage the church clergy in the world today, but I am talking directly about the heads of each religious institution at the top. The leaders who have access to the truth, but for reasons only known to those at the top, keep the status quo in place and the people in servitude to the church, and not to their inherit destiny.

Another word that is directly tied to the chakra system is the *Kundalini,* but the activation of the *Kundalini,* that is part of the spinal column, can only happen through our spiritual awareness and doing the work that is required to activate it.

Not knowing, that praying the right way, meditating the right way, and taking the time to align one's self with the (right) Most High God, through one's individual journey is like leaving you in the desert without water. The journey to the Most High God is just as important as breathing and to keep us uninformed is impeding both the individual and our collective growth. But again it does keep the status quo in place, which for those at the top, is most important.

The East teaches Yoga, if it is not your thing, meditate, if it is not your thing, try thinking of it another way; the bible says, "be still and know that I am God." So just be still, for as long as you can and as often as you can, and let the Most High God look into your center and let the Most High God breathe life into your center and watch your chakra system react favorably as you come into alignment. Although, it is will not be an overnight achievement, you will receive new opportunities to revisit past mistakes, and change the outcome from a negative to a positive, and with each good decision, your energy will flow, and provide much needed nourishment to the upper chakras, as you continue to climb *Jacob's ladder,* and leave one church for another.

The spiritual fire of the Kundalini is not easy activated but when it is, it has the power to activate the entire chakra system, which brings you into the realm of oneness. Yes it can be a great force for good within you, but it can also get stuck and become shut off from its upward flow. When one's focus is on the wrong thing, which is just the sexual nature of the activation, it becomes just a physical tool, and without the spiritual component, it becomes damaged and will not serve you well, without much repair work being done first.

Those operating in this way have problematic responses to the complexities of the world today and it is seem in the churches today. Some churches have completely gone off the rails and become subjected to the wrong ideals and motivations of the world's powers, which allowed deviate behavior, lowering of standards, closing of the circle, having judgmental ruling against any naysayers, and a complete lack of empathy for anyone outside the inner circle. Does any of this sound like the world of today?

If you are a member of such a church, just know that their spiritual growth has become stuck and there is nothing more to learn there. It is time to move away, as nothing nourishing is on their menu, for as in all things, actions speak louder than words.

But when the chakra system is functioning at its highest level and the Kundalini is fully activated and flowing with spiritual fire the bride and the Bride grown of Western thought is united and we are one with the Most High God. It can happen through a church or it can happen through your individual work, but understand this, each individual is responsible for their evolutionary growth and the ultimate attainment of oneness. We cannot get to the door of Grace and blame the church for not teaching us, we each have our own cross to bear and our own path to forge. Knowledge is power, get some, it will save your life.

Here are the Western Seven Churches and the Eastern Seven Chakras and their relationship to your body and your life's progression.

Here is where, the West finally meets the East, our path to enlightenment must include the Eastern teachings or we will miss out on the glory and true meaning of climbing Jacob's ladder.

This chart lined the Western Church and the Eastern Chakras up from the bottom of the spinal column, but in the human body you see them from the crown above the head down to the root. But rightly showing that before the energy can flow downward from the crown it must correctly have uninterrupted flow upward from the root. Much like a tree's roots the chakra must be nourished before branches can grow leaves or continue to branch out.

Blending the Western and Eastern Chakra System

Church Name	Chakra Name	Spinal Column Area	Spinal Region Location	Color Vibration	Sound Vowel Vibration
Ephesus	Root	Fear/Desire	L5-S5	Red	UUH
Smyrna	Sacrum/ Navel	Feelings	T9-L4	Orange	OOO
Pergamos	Adrenal Gland/ Solar Plexus	Proactivity	T5-T9	Yellow	OH
Thyatira	Heart	Harmony	T1-5	Green	AH
Sardis	Thyroid Gland	Throat/ Philosophy	C3-7	Blue	EYE
Philadelphia	Pituitary Gland	Third Eye/ Wisdom	C1-2	Indigo	AYE
Laodicea	Pineal Gland	Crown/ Spirituality	Carotid/ Pineal Gland	Violent	EEE

In the year 2007 I became aware that one could increase the energy flow of their spinal column through Chiropractic Subluxation. It was said to increase the energy flow throughout the body and thereby decrease the chances of future problems and as well as provide good energy to problem areas. I am probably not explaining this very well but it was my understanding at the time I started going for the Subluxation adjustments.

I am so happy that I did. It was a wonderful experience, easy to do and has given me many years of good energy flow, which I am sure has been a great benefit to my overall health and well-being.

When, West meets East, the many things that God intended us to know and utilize will become available for our continued enjoyment of planet earth.

Prayer and meditation

We in the West call it prayer and in the East it is called meditation, and they are performed very differently. When we pray, we talk to God and at the end we say amen and go about the business of whatever our daily lives has placed on us. But when we meditate we enter into a state of silence, so that the mind of God can commune with our spiritual over-self without the inference of the physical mind and will.

The West and the East approach their relationship very differently; the West thinks talking, pleading, asking, bargaining, demanding, cajoling and lying during prayer is the way to get the job done, and then so many will say that prayer does not work, I really can't imagine why. The East can teach us this simple thing, forget the words and bring your heart, the very aura of your body the colors of your chakra system tells the Holy Spirit everything that is needed to be known. Words are completely unnecessary to know what is best for your highest good. There is an old saying, "You may not get what you want, but you can get what you need." I am convinced that through your willingness to meditate, and just let your heart be examined, that the very best for your future well-being will be manifested at the right time.

Of course there are many that teach how to meditate and many that teach how to pray, and either one will work, for through it all, it does not matter what you say, the chakra system of the body will show where your attention has been placed and where your upward mobility has become stuck.

Therefore no matter who wants to teach you, it will still come down to a one-on-one relationship in which your heart holds all of the keys, and your actions control all of your progress.

The Lazarus Effect

Before the Chakra System can be fully activated the *Lazarus Effect* has to come into play.

The density of the earth's environment and the ability for humans to sink deep into the depths of its atmosphere will require the *Lazarus Effect* for some and the *Christ Effect* for others.

In the *Christ Effect* it took three days for the resurrection of the Christ to take place and those like the Christ will be renewed in the metaphorical three days of time. But those who have sank lower into the depths of their existence, whose bodies are described as Lazarus's body was as badly rotten, it will take a metaphoric four days of time to bring them forward and out o the depths of darkness.

The bible talks of the many times those resurrection occurrences took place but Lazarus was different, and I think it is directly related to the time of 12-12-12 and the coming end of the age.

There are writings of how the Christ went deep into the bowels of hell to bring all the souls out for the final judgment. This would indeed require a different agenda, and it would indeed have to be set apart.

This is a set-a-part in our existence of time; it is an opportunity to get it right; it is an opportunity to take charge of our destiny and to effect change in our lives for the better. No more ground hog lives, we can understand that this time is different; that some of the people of earth are seen as having reached their lowest common denominator, and have caused the whole earth to be in need of an course correction in a so to speak "come to Jesus moment", point in time.

We are about to have our *Lazarus Effect* for with it is the full blown calling of all souls. Whichever terminology describes your life, it will be resurrection time for all. Whatever turmoil it will put you through, is a part of the process we will all have to go through, and because we are all creatures of habit, this will definitely take us outside our comfort zone, but toward the light.

"Which I am sure will make it all worth it in the end, hallelujah!"

After doing the hard work we can graduate with honors and be ready to enter the new world with credentials behind our name, and knowledge, understanding and wisdom in our head.

The Raising of the Dead

The raising of the dead in the bible (resurrection experience)
1 Kings 17:17-24 (KJV)
A son was raised from the dead by Elijah the prophet whom I consider an earlier Christ from another dispensation of time.
2 Kings 4:18-37 (KJV)
The prophet Elisha raised a son from the dead remember he was the one who wanted to follow Elijah, and is considered to possibility be the Christ of the dispensation after Elijah. Of this I am not convinced. There is no real evidence to support this that I have found.
Luke 7:11-17
Another son was raised from the dead by Jesus.
Luke 8:52-56
A *daughter* was raised by Jesus this is turning point in the evolutionary path of humankind, and to not to be missed, for it portends something, that has been over shadowed by the resurrection itself.
John 11

- It tells of the third person raised from the dead, by Jesus, in a very different way. Some relevant facts to look closely at are:
- It was the third person, the number three always has significance whenever it show up in the bible
- Bethany is mentioned as the home of Mary and Martha
- It was the fourth day
- John 11:4 states that he said, *"this sickness is not unto death, but for the glory of God that the Son of God, might be glorified thereby."*
- John 25 states "I am the resurrection and the life: he that believeth in me, though he were dead, yet shall he live "

To me this means that it was done to prove a point.
Lazarus was buried in a cave; a dark place, his body stank from the rotting condition that his flesh was in.
Spiritual symbolism proves that no matter how low we can and have sank into the depths of the earth, no matter how far away from the spiritual light of God, the darkness cannot completely shut out the light, and as long as there is a spark of light, there is a way to roll away the stone that shuts the cave we might find ourselves locked in, for there is no entrance that the Glory of God cannot not open and enter.
John 11:43
And Jesus said *"Lazarus come forth!"*
During the coming dispensation of time this will occur, and those who were dead in Christ will rise.

John11:52
And not for that nation only, but that also he should gather together in one the children of God that were scattered abroad. (KJV)

Because this brought fear to those in power, it was determined that the Christ should die for the people, not just those there but for all the children of God that are scattered abroad. Did we miss this, they are openly saying that the followers of Christ are the children of God, how is it, I am just now seeing this fully, with eyes wide open, for the first time?

John 11:52-54
[52] And not for that nation only, but that also he should gather together in one the children of God that were scattered abroad.
[53] Then from that day forth they took counsel together for to put him to death.
[54] Jesus therefore walked no more openly among the Jews; but went thence unto a country near to the wilderness, into a city called Ephraim, and there continued with his disciples.

Jesus went unto a country near the wilderness call Ephraim, and spent time with his disciples.

I place no credence on the raising of the dead <u>by the disciples</u> as written in other passages of the bible. It doesn't quite fit with the deeper meaning of the truth of resurrection power. However if it feels right to you, that okay too, our journey continues. We are all by now seeker of truth.

The *Lazarus* story speaks of an entirely different circumstance than the normal three day resurrection of the Christ and Christ like first fruits or the chosen, which has a three day <u>trinity-type</u> resurrection. But the Lazarus resurrection required a different process within a different timeframe to bring him forth.

What does Bethany represent?
- The biblical meaning of Bethany is house of figs; figs in the bible represent un-ripened fruit; a place of spiritual poverty

What does Ephraim represent?
- Ephraim was one of the twelve tribes of Israel; Ephraim received the blessing of the firstborn; the meaning of Ephraim is fruitful

What does the number three represent?
- Resurrection took three full days
- Jesus prayed three times in the Garden of Gethsemane
- The number of Divine Perfection
- Omniscient, Omnipresent, and Omnipotent

- Past, present and future
- The use of thought, word and deed
- The use of mind, body and spirit

These and many more emphasize the importance placed on recognizing and placing great value on the number three. The old folks used to say, "If it comes in three's", they would place great importance on it, and so it has been throughout history.

What does the number four represent?

The number four gets it biblical meaning from creation which took place in the bible on the fourth day.

- The number four is the number for earth and humankind; it is also the number of wholeness and completion. It also denotes diversity.
- Things of earth are steeped in the number four
- The four phases of the moon
- The four corners of the earth
- The four seasons etc

The bible said that on the fourth day the day was divided from the night. This is so important, but I missed it again and again. Just think what the resurrection of Lazarus means being raised not on the third but on the fourth day so he could be separated from the night or from the darkness that had hold on his body. But, also that he originally can after the separation of the day and the night.

Genesis 1:18

and to govern the day and the night, and to separate the light from the darkness; and God saw that it was good.

Genesis 1:19

And the evening and the morning were the fourth day.

At the end of the dispensation there will indeed be a Lazarus Effect, and from the four corners of the earth, and from the depths of darkness all will rise, and receive their personal judgment, and their opportunity to participate in the *New Jerusalem*.

The Butterfly Effect

The butterfly Effect definition:
A noun the phenomenon whereby a minute localized change in a complex system can have large effects elsewhere.

The *Butterfly Effect* is closely related to the Chaos theory which is: *When the present determines the future, but the approximate present does not approximately determine the future* as summarized by Edward Lorenz.

This will be exactly what can happen and in my estimation what is happening now because of the times we are living in and the things we are experiencing.

The one thing, that the end times purveyors of our fate have in common is, that what happens at the end will happen to us all. The bible states that we will either be caught up or left-behind, and doomed to some kind of hell and brimstone fire eternal existence.

But, I contend and am convinced, that as eternal and saved individuals we have come by this at different times; and with different knowings' to know and with different experiences needed to grow, and spiral ever higher on our evolutionary journey. Therefore, it would be impracticable for us all too just interrupt the learning process and just ascend or be rejected, that in and of itself would cause chaos.

The *Butterfly Effect* could however change on an individual level ones' future projection according to where they are at a given dispensation and reckoning.

We as individuals have different experiences, different paths and different missions assigned to us to help propel the human existence forward, so as reset buttons go, no one will start over at square one. Also, no one will be forced to go somewhere they do not want to go. It will be their choice and it will be according to their conditional set of beliefs.

The more we know now, the better prepared we will be when the judgment is upon us.

When we have the full understanding, that you will be standing naked before the Throne figuratively speaking, and that there will be no need to plead your case, for the goodness or lack thereof has already been weighed, and the appropriate dispensation set from the fair and balanced Divine Energy of the Holy Spirit, whose love and mercy is tempered with fairness and justice. It will be enough just to say, "Thy will be done."

The entry of the Divine Holy Spirit and the Divine energy into our atmosphere has started the chaos, that the planet is experiencing right now as well as the physical chaos created by humankind's unwillingness to take care of Mother Earth.

The two chaotic situations together will set off a tidal wave of seemingly unrelated events that will cause the dispensation to occur. The biblical *Signs and Wonders* are all around us now. The bible correctly pointed to the conditions that will be occurring; just remember it is not on a macro scale, it all is happening on a micro scale at the individual level. We will all have our Armageddon and "our come to Jesus moment" because it is written.

You may not recognize the moment as such, and when you come through the storm, you may not realize what a major milestone it was in your life, but as your life gets better and new challenges arise, but it will serve you well to remember when times were worse and seek comfort in the here and now of your existence. For it was not you and you alone, that brought you this far.

Chapter Twenty-Four

Correlation of Divine Energy and Return the of the Feminine Spirit

I believe the Divine Energy will bring the energy we need to nourish and strengthen our hearts and keep us to become the givers of the fruits of the spirit as the main energy source that will prevail in the planet for as the bible says a thousand years.

We have no way of knowing what a thousand years really means, is it a thousand light years, is it a thousand times a thousand, or a million times a thousand? We don't know, and it really doesn't matter that we know only that we can't take it literally.

The true workings and understandings of The Divine Energy will never be known in words on paper. It is hard to grasp what one individually is able to feel, but it is impossible to articulate, for the reality of God is beyond comprehension and explanation.

But enter the maternal Mother Energy to feed her children from her breast with the ultimate mother's milk filled with all the qualities of the *Fruits of the Spirit*, to give all who received the *Butterfly Effect*, everything they need to grow expediently from where they are at that moment.

This will cause much chaos in the world as the end of the old order comes to an end. *They will not go quietly into that dark night.* But as love, awareness and righteousness rises up to usher in the glory of the "thousand years" and replace the negative thought forms with positive ones, the impact will cause a mass exodus to take place as the knowledge spreads that they are indeed outgunned, outnumbered and have lost the war to stay in charge.

The entrance of the powerful energy of the Most High God, to find her children and to nourish them with her loving energy, is essentially at the height of the tribulation period. The boundless blessing of the Most High God will rest upon her children and each in their own way will receive everything they need to continue their journey.

The earth will be revived as the *Butterfly Effect* puts good energy into every living thing so that the echo system is once again balanced and is returned to normal. The water will become clean and the air will become pure and the good earth will be replenished with good soil.

Everything that grows will become vibrant with colors that cause one to rethink the entire color spectrum. Everything will be complete once again, and full of whatever is needed according to its purpose.

This will be increasingly important as nature was designed to be the healer and in its' highest form quite adequate for our medical needs.

And as for humankind, those who are blessed to be alive during this time, you will feel as never before, love as never before, understand things as never before, and share all that you are as never before.

The children of the Most High God will have empathy for every living creature as they now know that there is a place for everything under the sun. This is a part of their re-knowing and a part of their stewardship of the earth.

The good stewards of the earth will now understand it is not about having power over any other beings or things, but in just being a good servant to each other and the abundance of what is provided on earth.

In the new world we will still have problems because people will always have free will, but we will also have help. It will not be a world controlled by separation through the use of "isms" but a world of love for one another. It will be a world of individual communication with the Most High God who provides the common denominator all will have that drink of the spiritual water.

Problems are meant to be solved with the help of others for the good of all, and in the new *Dispensation of Grace* it will be so.

We will experience a quantum leap in our evolutionary growth and with new advances in technology, medicine and science will catapult us further than we could ever imagine into the future.

The Keys of Enoch tells of scientific advances that are way beyond my comprehension to understand but do foretell of the quantum leap we will experience. I choose to believe it to be so, for the information would not have been presented to me to share with you. I have had this information for some fifteen years, just waiting for the right time.

We are truly multidimensional beings and in this new dimension we will learn to dwell simply while at the same time creating everything we need when we need it.

As multidimensional beings we will be able to also help other dimensions by incorporating advances we have into their processes as they are able to understand, comprehend and accept the gifts we bring.

With the darkness diminished and the love of our Mother strong and infused in our lives, we will continue to grow in grace and mercy and continue to do the work of the "chosen" and yes the work of the "saved."

It is not that darkness will have ceased to exist, but it is a dimensional thing and as you are able to go from one dimension to another the darkness is further diminished, and your ability to attract, retain, and experience the light becomes greater and greater. When you are armed with the light your opportunities to grow and you will be able to connect on an even deeper level with the Most High God, this will also increase your ever evolving path, which will continue to excite and bring joy to your existence and to everything around you.

The Book of Revelation

Revelation 3:20-22
Behold, I stand at the door, and knock: if any man hear my voice, and open the door, I will come in to him, and will sup with him, and he with me.
To him that overcometh will I grant to sit with me in my throne, even as I also overcame, and am set down with my Father in his throne.
He that hath an ear, let him hear what the Spirit saith unto the churches.

Revelation 21:1-2
And I saw a new heaven and a new earth: for the first heaven and the first earth were passed away; and there was no more sea.[2] And I John saw the holy city, new Jerusalem, coming down from God out of heaven, prepared as a bride adorned for her husband
Revelation 21:22-23
And I saw no temple therein: for the Lord God Almighty and the Lamb are the temple of it.
And the city had no need of the sun, neither of the moon, to shine in it: for the glory of God did lighten it, and the Lamb is the light thereof.
Revelation 21:27
Only those whose names are written in the Lamb's book will inter the city.
Wow, according to the end of the bible it is only the Lamb's book that counts when you want to enter the New Jerusalem (the city) at the beginning of the new dispensation period.

But, on another note...
I can agree that these are all great passages full of hope and optimism about the new future we will embrace in the coming of new time. However, all of these passages are overshadowed by the incorrect metaphor used to describe the evil system that plagued those of earth by the masculine patriarchal system.

AN HONEST DISCUSSION IS NEEDED HERE...

Taken verbatim from the www.discoverrelevation.com

No system in the world's history has enslaved more people than this awful religion. It should not take us by surprise that this prostitute woman, the religious system, is referred to as a city. When used symbolically, a woman is always intended throughout the Scripture to signify a spiritual or religious movement. If a good woman, it is "Jehovah's wife" or "the bride of Christ". If an evil woman, such as "a prostitute," it represents the evil religious system of idolatry.

Since the woman who rides the beast gets her authority from the beast, the Holy Spirit uses this description to show how religious Babylon and governmental Babylon are so intertwined they are presented together. However, they are destroyed at different times. The prostitute (religious Babylon) is destroyed by "beast and the kings of the earth," who "hate the prostitute" and kill her. This clears the way for Antichrist to fulfill the lifetime dream of Satan to get people to worship him. She is destroyed in the middle of the Tribulation; Babylon the governmental system will be destroyed at the end, when commercial, political Babylon is destroyed (Rev. 18). With "Mystery Babylon, the Mother of Prostitutes" out of the way, "all inhabitants of the earth will worship the beast, all whose names have not been written in the book of life belonging to the Lamb that was slain from the creation of the world". (Rev. 13 v.8)

The Vision of the Woman - Ten details describe this woman:
1. *The great prostitute*
2. *Who sits on many waters*
3. *With her the kings of the earth committed adultery.*
4. *The inhabitants of the earth were intoxicated with the wine of her adulteries.*
5. *A woman sitting on a scarlet beast*
6. *Dressed in purple and scarlet*
7. *Glittering with gold, precious stones and pearls*
8. *She held a golden cup in her hand, filled with abominable things and the filth of her adulteries.*
9. *On her forehead: Mystery Babylon the Great, the Mother of Prostitutes and of the Abomination of the Earth.*
10. *Drunk with the blood of the saints, the blood of those who bore testimony to Jesus*

Even before we come to the angel's interpretation of this vision, it is clear that we are not dealing with a mere human being, for no one woman can commit fornication with the kings of the earth, nor can a woman be "drunk with the blood of the saints, the blood of those who bore testimony to Jesus."

The literal interpretation of these passages has served to denigrate women and make them second and third class citizens down through the ages.

To make our mother a metaphorical evil symbol in the bible is in and of itself disgraceful, but to not explain in great detail that it is a poor use of symbolism is even worse. It has caused a total disregard for the welfare and well-being of entirely too many women around the world and instead of the equality of all it has led to a world that not only do males have dominion over the beast of the field but over women as well. Therefore, instead of seeing women as equal helpmates, far too many were seen as servants to their masters, and often treated as disposable.

Where was our compassion, where was our honesty and where is the moral compass today?

The Great Mother, the Most High God wept and rivers and oceans were formed to provide separation from the pain of such hurt.

Yet, she, the Divine Mother Energy, since the beginning chose love and now we too much chose LOVE! Nothing less will do.

The bottom line…

Hallelujah everyone the end has finally come and the beginning is almost here.

The Christ will come and with him the 144,000 chosen will join him

The cross you must bear will appear for your understanding

Then as this phase has concluded and your full judgment and comprehension noted

The Christ will proclaim

"Behold your Mother" and if you do, the Divine Energy will enter for all who accept and the real saying "out of one many!" will be true. And you will enter your new earth and your new heaven, which will be uniquely yours, dimensionally speaking.

Yes, it will be a Hallelujah time in the land.

Behold!

Chapter Twenty-Five

The Divine Grace of the Mother

T he free and unmerited favor of God, as it is manifested in the
salvation of sinners, and the bestowal of blessings.

Unmerited divine assistance given humans for their regeneration
or sanctification

A virtue coming from God; a state of sanctification enjoyed
through divine grace

I think we can safely say that the bestowal of Grace on an entire
planet has not happened during our known or recorded history. It seems
that the only time such Grace was bestowed to our knowing was in the
Garden of Eden, and even that did not last.

But at the same time there are religious scholars that write that we
are currently in the Dispensation of Grace. You see the definition of grace,
what planet are they living in if they think that we are currently living in
such a period?

What would the 99% have to look forward to, if we were already
living the best way we could have?

I can understand it only from another point of view; a point of
view that just may have some standing.

What if the scholars were talking to a group of people not the
entire population? What if it really is the grace period of the rich, the
famous and the powerful; and what if it was nearing the end of their
reign? That would make sense and would certainly agree with my
timeframe for the coming dispensation of the return of Grace.

When it cannot be bought and paid for in the normal business
transaction sense what does the ruling elite have to bargain with?

When money, looks and power are off the table, what will they
have to offer to Divine Energy in return for a good place in the new
dispensation of Grace?

The definition of the dispensation of Grace is described as if it is
the time we are living in today, but we now know that this not true. If it
was the time of Grace, it would not have the poor be forgotten and
charged for being poor, while the rich kept getting richer off the backs of
the poor.

No I say, this is not the time of Grace, it is coming and it is coming soon, when the Divine Mother sends her loving energy to combat and win over the energies of darkness and subdue her most ardent opponents, then my friends we will truly enter the Dispensation of Grace.

Grace responds to the *Chakra System*, not to money, position or power. The energy of correspondence, *the Laws of Attraction* will definitely come into play here as all energy will be in play.

Some will continue to be angry but many more will succumb to joy and the blissful peace that will inhabit their sphere. The chores of daily living will not change, but the attitude and effort needed to accomplish a task will make the burdens lighter.

The heaviness of heart will be lifted and the joy of being alive will make one see possibilities not seen or known about before as achievable.

We will enter the real Dispensation of Grace, no false pretenses, no false gods, no false intermediate intercessors; we will come to the Mother each one at their own pace and each with their own understanding.

We will be under the Grace, the Mercy, and the Protection of Our Mother, the energy of all the spheres that extends from beyond the unknown vast universes to our small planet call Earth.

We will be blessed nurtured and allowed to grow in the Grace of the period that we will indeed become our fullest self and realize our fullest potential.

This is your inheritance!

Chapter Twenty-Six

I leave you with....

Mark 8:22-26
And he cometh to Bethsaida; and they bring a blind man unto him, and besought him to touch him.

The place Bethsaida has significance because of the name and the biblical location of where it is said to reside.

But the real word is "blind", being blind in the bible is not always a literal term, it can also mean that it happened by no fault, or by disobedience, or ignorance of spiritual things. In this particular case, I think it is the latter, for this story is used as a teaching moment and a foretelling of events to come.

And he took the blind man by the hand, and led him out of the town; and when he had spit on his eyes, and put his hands upon him, he asked him if he saw ought.

Bethsaida was on the wrong side of the Jordan, so Jesus led him away, very important knowing here.

And he looked up, and said, I see men as trees, walking.

He asked him what he saw and his first answer gave Christ the information he sought, that he saw men rooted in the ways of the earth, but saw nothing wrong with it.

After that he put his hands again upon his eyes, and made him look up: and he was restored, and saw every man clearly.

Now having spiritual sight, he was able to see that there was nothing spiritual in the men he saw clearly.

And he sent him away to his house, saying, neither go into the town, nor tell it to any in the town.

This knowledge wasn't for everyone to know, for it was not time to this to occur. It was an awakening that could be given to many when and if the time was right. Therefore he was told to stay away from the place where men were like trees, and tell no one what he saw.

The bible continues to amaze and exalt the seeker. Be a seeker!

Seek your place in the universe and your rightful place in the kingdom of The Most High God.

Recapping!

Chapter Twenty-Seven

Recapping the Book…

T hroughout, I have tried to convey some conclusions I have
arrived at during my search to re-know all that I possess within me.

Using the vast resources of the universe, the Akaskic Records, the
wonderful access to the Thoughtland, and my amazing home library of
books collected with the help of the universe and people put in my path to
help with my awakening.
I have presented some basic truths that I hope you will consider in the
course of your awakening, which are designed to further you along your
path of individual discovery of the Most High God.
They are that:

The bible is older than the dirt of this earth, and can be accessed on
a deeper more meaningful level, once you become a seeker of truth.

There are definitions behind words and phrases that the average
person has not been told behind every literal interpretation in the bible.

The literal interpretation of the bible is just a story, which has no
basis in historical timelines and facts.

The words, phrases, parables and stories in the bible all have
hidden knowing designed to be discovered to enhance not hinder your
spiritual growth.

There was a deliberate removable of the feminine aspect from the
bible, and a replacement of references of the masculine.

Our direct relationship with God was replaced with our direct
relationship and allegiance to the church.

We have not been told how important it is to address our God as
the Most High God because of all the demigods and false gods that are in
abundance on the planet, seeking our attention, with promises of
grandeur.

The bible continues to reveal its secrets, no matter how well
hidden and deleted from the bible they may be.

We live in a multidimensional world and have the ability to move
from dimension to dimension depending on our spiritual progression in
life.

By not incorporating Eastern spiritual thought with Western religious though we have received an incomplete roadmap of the path to God, health, well-being and happiness.

Hell is not a physical place but a mental state of mind, body, spirit and soul that manifest itself into the environment one finds oneself in as they succumb to the attachments of darkness.

The timeframe of 12-12-12 was indeed marking the end of one dispensation to make way for a new one to come.

The time is right to look for signs and wonders, for the things that are coming will be hard to miss.

The "chosen", "Elected", and "Sealed" had a very important reason for being and a unique history which has never been correctly taught or known by major Western religious traditions.

There is no such thing as "blood of Unknown Origin", just scientist that could not combine the laws of science with the truth of religion to determine the origin.

The awakening of the Children of the Light and their re-knowing will help usher in the return.

The re-knowing is upon us. A time when we will rekindle our relationship with the Divine Mother and receive the Fruits of the Spirit to re-nourish our battered beings, that we may spread Light, Love, and Joy across the planet.

There are new and wondrous times ahead with bright days as the old warring masculine energy gives way to the Divine Feminine, and love, joy, peace, patience, kindness, goodness, and faithfulness of the Divine Tree will be made available for all that enter into Her Love.

Just as morning breaks through the darkness and shines bright for all to see, so will the Divine Light of the Most High God shine through the darkness and give hope to the hopeless and opportunity to rise out of dark places to all that have the will to do so.

The Divine Feminine Energy of the Beloved Iconic Mother will once again be with her Iconic child.

The Iconic child correctly represents that out of one is many.

Let those that have eyes to see and ears to hear enter into their rightful place and assist all of humankind to do the same.

Amen!

Selah!

Namaste!

Ashe!

And so it is!

Selected References**

The Holy Bible King James Version

The Interpreter's Bible, A Commentary of Volumes 2, 5, 10, Abingdon Press, Nashville, Tennessee, 1953

The New Interpreter's Bible – A Commentary in Twelve Volumes, Abingdon Press, Nashville, Tennessee Volumes 1-12, 1994-1998

The Gnostic Gospel of St. Thomas – Meditations on the Mystical Teachings, Tau Malachi, Llewellyn Publications, St. Paul Minnesota, 2004

The Gospel of Thomas – The Gnostic Wisdom of Jesus, Jean-Yves Leloup, Inner Traditions, Rochester, Vermont, 1986

Authentic spirituality – The direct Path to consciousness, Richard N. Potter, Llewellyn Publications, St. Paul Minnesota, 2004

Living Gnosis – a practical Gu9de to Gnostic Christianity, Tau Malachi, Llewellyn Publications, Woodbury Minnesota, 1962

The Gospel of Philip – Jesus, Mary Magdalene, and the Gnosis of Sacred Union, Jean-Yves Leloup, Inner Traditions, Rochester, Vermont, 2004

Gnostic secrets of the Naassenes – the Initiatory Teachings of the Last Super, mark H. Gaffney, Inner Traditions, Rochester, Vermont, 2004

The Gospel of John – In the Light of Indian Mysticism, Ravi Ravindra, Ph.D., inner Traditions, Rochester, Vermont, 2004

The Jerusalem Bible Reading Edition, Doubleday & Company, Garden City, New York, 1968

The Decoded new Testament – The sacred Teachings of Light, Codex II, Volume I, The International Community of Christ, Reno, Nevada, 1975

Bible Code, Michael Drosnin, Simon & Schuster, 1997

Bible Code II, Michael Drosnin, Penguin Group, 2002

The Dead Sea Scrolls – A New Translation, Michael Wise, martin Abegg, Jr., Edward Cook, Harper Collins Publishers, 1996

The Odes of Solomon: Original Christianity Revealed, Dr. Robert Winterhalter, Llewellyn Publications, St. Paul Minnesota, 1985

Lost Books of Bible – and the forgotten books of Eden, World Bible Publishers, Inc., Alpha House, Inc. 1926

The Emerald Tablet of Hermes, and the Kybalion – Two Classic books on Hermetic Philosophy, Edited by Dr. Jaes Ma'ati Smith C.Hyp. Msc.D. 2008

The Uranta Book, Uranta Foundation, Chicago, Illinois, 1995

The Book of Knowledge – The Keys of Enoch, J.J. Hurtak, The Academy of future Science, 1973

Pistis Sophia – A Coptic Text of Gnosis Commentary, J.J. Hurtak Ph.D., M.th., Desiree Hurtak, MS Sc, The Academy of Future Science, 2003

The Sermon on the Mount – The Keys of success in Life, Emmit Fox, Harper Collins Publishers, 1989

The lost Years of Jesus – Documentary evidence of 27-year journey to the East, Elizabeth Clare Prophet, summit University Press, Corwin Springs, Montana, 1984

The Illustrated World Religions – a guide to our wisdom traditions, Huston Smith, Harper Collins Publishers, 1958

Great Religions of the World, National Geographic Society, 1971

Sophia – Maria- A Holistic Vision of Creation, Thomas Schipflinger, translated by James Margante, Samuel Weiser, Inc. York Beach, Maine, 1998

The Sirius Mystery – was earth visited by intelligent beings from a planet in the system of the Star Sirius? Robert K. G. Temple, St Martin's Pres, 1976

African Exodus – origins of modern humanity, Christoper Stringer and robin McKie

A Book of the Beginnings Volumes I & II, Gerald Massey, University Books, Inc. Secaucus, New Jersey, 1974

Stolen Legacy, George G. M. James, Philosophical Library, New York, 1954

Golden Age of the Moor, Ivan Van Sertima, transaction Publishers, New Brunswick, 1992

** These references are all foundational, my research was unlimited in scope but they did provide a great opening of the mind and useful reference points in my search to uncover the truth.

About the Author

Gwyndolyn D. Parker is a retired professional who dreamed of becoming a journalist as a high school student, but instead in college majored in computer science with a minor in business, and spent an entire career utilizing those skills. However, her dreams of becoming a writer did not die, and dreams do come true. Writing is now her new pastime, and her second chance of realizing her dreams.

She spent many years working in the community on matters of diversity and race relations. During those years she was trained by noted diversity organization and much of her social justice thinking was formulated during those years.

Her interest in spirituality led her to seek counsel with Metaphysical Universal Ministries where she became an ordained minister and teacher of spiritual studies in their ordination programs.

She has always been a student of the news, and how it relates to the African American experience; how it has been recorded in history is now, for her, more than a pastime, it is a major part of the research needed for future books.

Her latest Self Published Books Include:

2012 – The Systematic Denial of the American Dream
2012 – The Unseen Advantage in the Wings of Black Women
2014 – My Shrink Asked Me What I Was Thinking: this is what I told him!
2016 – Coffee, Tea and Conversation
2016 – Gwynisms II

www.ingramcontent.com/pod-product-compliance
Lightning Source LLC
Chambersburg PA
CBHW021139090426
42740CB00008B/851